America's First Negro Poet
The Complete Works of
Jupiter Hammon of Long Island

THE LLOYD MANOR HOUSE
Photograph by Carl Anderson Through the Courtesy of the
Lloyd Harbour Historical Commission

AMERICA'S FIRST NEGRO POET

The Complete Works of

JUPITER HAMMON *of* LONG ISLAND

Edited with an Introduction by
STANLEY AUSTIN RANSOM, JR.

Biographical Sketch of Jupiter Hammon by
OSCAR WEGELIN

Critical Analysis of the Works of Jupiter Hammon by
VERNON LOGGINS

Ira J. Friedman Division
KENNIKAT PRESS
Port Washington, N.Y.

EMPIRE STATE HISTORICAL PUBLICATIONS SERIES
No. 82

Biographical Sketch first published in *Jupiter Hammon*, American Negro Poet by Oscar Wegelin. New York 1915. Critical Analysis first published in *The Negro Author:* His Development in America to 1900 by Vernon Loggins. Port Washington, N.Y. 1964.

To my wife

Dorothy

CONTENTS

An Important Note Concerning
Jupiter Hammon's Birthday

The exact birthdate of Jupiter Hammon has at last been discovered. The day is October 17, 1711, and it appears in Henry Lloyd's handwriting in a list of birth dates of his slaves. Credit for the discovery of this list in the back of a Lloyd ledger in the archives of the Long Island Historical Society goes to Mrs. Lillian Koppel, a graduate student in the American Studies class of Professor Louis Lomax of Hofstra University.

Since this important discovery was made after the manuscript of this book was already set into type, the Publisher is pleased to provide the information in this informal way.

INTRODUCTION

by Stanley Austin Ransom, Jr.

The three white dormer windows of Lloyd Manor House peer through the limbs of the tall locust trees and look out over the reed-edged shores and the placid waters of Lloyd Harbor on Long Island's northern shore. Its unique history endows the three-storied structure with an air of regal mystery, and its paneled walls still seem to echo from the sounds of lords and ladies, merchants and princes, patriots and Tories. The unusual character of the house is more fully revealed as the tale unfolds of its secret passageway and the hidden opening in the upper room. Twelve British soldiers are said to have escaped the wrath of local patriots by creeping through this tunnel to the harbor and the safety of their ships during the American Revolution. This historic residence of the Lloyd family has been acquired by the Society for the Preservation of Long Island Antiquities but it will continue as a private residence not open to visitors for a few years. It will eventually be opened to the public as a house of considerable historic merit.

Lloyd Manor House also shares a claim to literary fame, for the Manor was the home of Jupiter Hammon, credited with being the first American Negro to publish poetry. He lived and died as a slave in the Lloyd family in the eighteenth century. The pre-eminence of Jupiter Hammon as the first American Negro poet rests upon the publication of four poems, the first being *An Evening Thought,* published in broadside form and dated December 25, 1760. Four prose pieces were also published, and of the eight items, only one, *An Essay on the Ten Virgins,* has not come to light.

11

The complete extant writings of Hammon appear in this volume in addition to Oscar Wegelin's lasting contribution to the body of knowledge about him, *Jupiter Hammon; American Negro Poet*. Few persons have had an opportunity to examine Wegelin's work, issued as it was in a special limited edition in 1915, and Wegelin's study is almost the sole authority on this black poet of Long Island.

Jupiter Hammon, who was born a slave, and who lived and died as a slave in the Lloyd family, deserves to be recognized for his contribution to early Afro-American culture. His poetry is sincere and enthusiastic, and is primarily religious. Hammon's poetry reflects his great intellectual and emotional involvement with religion, to the point where it approaches intoxication. It would seem likely that he was strongly affected by the renaissance of religious fervor which swept Long Island in the middle of the eighteenth century, for he expresses the deep evangelical feelings of the time. Yet the medium and the form of expression, while owing much to the poetic forms of the hymn writers, is his own, with stirring similarities to Negro spirituals and to other religious folk poetry. So intent is he upon his Christian message that the words and expressions are forced into verse mold almost as a procrustean endeavor.

His later prose unquestionably served the cause of freedom, for it pictures a Heaven in which white and black are equal and are judged alike. The spiritual equality of slave and master are strongly set forth in his *Address to the Negroes in the State of New-York*. He says, "The same God will judge both them and us," and "He will bring us all, rich and poor, white and black, to his judgment seat."

It is not surprising that this address, which must have dealt a blow to whites expounding a system of slavery based on a belief in racial superiority, was reprinted in 1787 by the Pennsylvania Society for Promoting the Abolition of Slavery. In this same address Hammon delivers arguments in favor of the abolition of slavery, and he states that he "would be glad if others, especially the young Negroes, were to be free." How ironic, he writes, that slavery should exist at the same time that the white people are spending their money and losing their lives for the cause of liberty in the American Revolution! For himself, a man of over seventy, he does not wish freedom, as he would "hardly know how to take care of himself," but he acknowledges that "liberty is a great thing, and worth seeking for."

The facts about Jupiter Hammon's early life, education and training are limited. The Lloyd estate, located on Long Island's North Shore, occupied the peninsula of Lloyd's Neck, between Oyster Bay and Huntington. Henry Lloyd, who rebuilt in 1722 the 1711 version of Lloyd Manor House, owned several Negro slaves needed to maintain the considerable property and enterprises of a prosperous merchant. One of these slaves was Jupiter Hammon, born in 1712,[1] possibly in New York City.[2] Except for a few years during the American Revolution, Hammon resided on the Lloyd estate until his death sometime after 1790.

On this estate Jupiter Hammon received his education along with other children living on the Manor. A small school was erected in Queen's Village, as the Manor was called between 1685 and 1790, and the instruction was supplied by the Lloyd family, or by schoolmasters such as Nehemiah Bull,[3] a Harvard graduate later to become a noted New England divine.

No information has come to light as to Hammon's duties and responsibilities, but later Hammon says that he was "able to do almost any kind of business." Langston Hughes states, "Hammon was an intelligent and privileged slave, respected by his master for his skill with tools and by his fellow slaves for his power as a preacher."[4] Whether as a house servant, artisan or student, he must have been very familiar with the Lloyd Manor House.

Not only did Hammon receive a better education than the

average slave, but he was probably allowed to use the library of Lloyd Manor House. Works of Burkitt and Bishop Beverage, great divines alluded to by Hammon, are known to have been part of the library of Henry Lloyd.[5]

In May 1733 Jupiter Hammon purchased from his master, for seven shillings and sixpence, a Bible with Psalms.[6] That this youthful servant was able to purchase this Bible and perhaps other books is an indication that Jupiter was able to earn some independent income and to devote some time to reading.

Upon the decease of Henry Lloyd in 1763, Hammon became the property of Joseph Lloyd, an American patriot. When Lloyd fled from the approaching British Army, his family and slaves accompanied him to Stamford, Connecticut, and later to Hartford.

Hammon's next four works were published in Hartford, then the literary capital of the Colonies. *An Address to Miss Phillis Wheatly* appeared in 1778, the elusive *Essay on the Ten Virgins* in 1779, *A Winter Piece* in 1782, and in the spring of 1783, the undated *An Evening's Improvement.*

During this time tragedy had come to the exiled Lloyd family. In June, 1780, Joseph Lloyd, hearing of the surrender of Charlestown, and believing it to be fact, thought the American cause was lost, and in a despondent mood took his own life.[7] The effect upon the family must have been devastating. It was as great for Jupiter Hammon, for it meant a new master, John Lloyd, Joseph's grandson, and a return to the Lloyd Manor.

Overton's *Long Island's Story* states that in 1782 Hammon composed a set of verses, not yet found and possibly not published, to celebrate the visit of young Prince William Henry, later King William IV, to Lloyd Manor House.[8] This was the first visit to America by any member of the British royal family, and the Prince, then called Duke of Clarence, displayed a lively and democratic temperment which delighted

Jupiter Hammon. The Prince visited nearby Fort Franklin accompanied by its designer, Colonel Benjamin Thompson, later Count Rumford, who together with other officers from the Fort was residing in Lloyd Manor House.

Jupiter Hammon's last work, *An Address to the Negroes in the State of New-York,* was published in 1787, with Hammon noted as "servant of John Lloyd, jun., Esq." in Queen's Village.

Exactly when Jupiter Hammon died or where his burial plot is located are unknown. It is probable that he died at Lloyd Neck and was buried in one of the plots of ground reserved for slaves. Headstones from many of these graves have disintegrated over the years. Oscar Wegelin was unable to find any trace of Hammon's grave, and recent attempts have also proven unsuccessful.

Bibliographic material on Jupiter Hammon is very slight. He was largely ignored by writers of the nineteenth century and he was probably unknown to those writers listing the achievements of other black writers. In contrast, the name of Phyllis Wheatly is often mentioned, perhaps due as much to her celebrated correspondence with George Washington as to her poetry.

To Oscar Wegelin must go the credit for discovering Jupiter Hammon and bringing him to the attention of the world. In rebutting a statement that Phyllis Wheatley was America's first Negro poet, Wegelin introduced Jupiter Hammon in an article "Was Phillis Wheatley America's First Negro Poet?" in the *Literary Collector* for August, 1904, but lacked, at that time, the necessary proof. Upon obtaining the necessary documentation Oscar Wegelin produced his *Jupiter Hammon; American Negro Poet,* thus backing up his claim and at the same time providing an extensive treatment of the Long Island slave-poet.

Wegelin's book has been the basis for most of the articles appearing in reference books and periodicals. Benjamin

Brawley contributed an excellent two-column treatment of Hammon in the *Dictionary of American Biography*, and he acknowledged the Wegelin account to be the most accessible source and practically the sole authority on Hammon. Brawley also considered the contribution of Hammon to Negro literature in his *Early Negro American Writers*, published in 1935.[9] He credits Hammon's *Address to the Negroes* with helping to influence later New York State legislation to abolish slavery within the State of New York.

The best critical treatment of Hammon's poetry is offered by Vernon Loggins in his *The Negro Author, His Development in America to 1900*.[10] Loggins acknowledges Hammon's unique contribution to American poetry in the eighteenth century, calling his verse the precursor of the Negro spiritual and remarkable for its touch of originality. Loggins' appraisal of Hammon is presented later in this volume preceding Hammon's poetry.

Reverend Charles A. Vertanes offers some revealing information about Hammon in his *Jupiter Hammon, Early Long Island Poet*, appearing in the Winter, 1957, issue of the *Nassau County Historical Journal*. This seventeen page study was based upon original research in the archives of the Long Island Historical Society, which holds many unpublished papers and account books of the Lloyd family. Rev. Vertanes discusses Hammon as a religious poet and also contributes much to the understanding of the early influence upon Hammon. This study is particularly useful in setting forth what is known about Hammon's schooling and reading. Henry Lloyd owned a fine library and had a strong desire to dispense knowledge, even importing books for sale, and he was generous in lending and in giving books to his friends and tenants. Hammon would have benefitted from such access to books and must have flourished in the intellectual atmosphere of Lloyd Manor House.

Other books of reference such as the *International Library of Negro Life and History* usually include a one column, unsigned, popular treatment of Jupiter Hammon. While most of these are brief and general, the one above offers the unsupported statement that Hammon was born in New York City. Hammon is sometimes described as being "unpopular among many of his race because of the acceptance of the role which life had placed upon him." His peers did not seem to appreciate the fact that Jupiter Hammon was an advocate of liberty for his race, even though he himself did not wish to be free. Considering that this statement was made when Hammon's age was in excess of seventy years, it is not surprising that he should choose the comfort which a kind master could give him in these later years.

An informative history of the slavery system and the abolition movement in New York State appears in Edgar J. McManus' book, *A History of Negro Slavery in New York,* published in 1966.[11] In the eighteenth century the arguments and attacks of missionaries and other religious leaders were very effective in halting the spread of slavery in New York State. The laws of New York State which curtailed slavery, freed some classes of slaves and which restricted the manumission of aged slaves, were passed in the 1780's, when Jupiter Hammon was in his seventies.

With the growing awareness of the Negro contributions to American literature, there are a number of articles urging the review of American literature and the teaching of a respect for the contributions of both black and white authors. One of these which mentions Jupiter Hammon is written by an educator, Carolyn Reese, in her article *From Jupiter Hammon to LeRoi Jones,* appearing in *Changing Education,* Fall, 1966.[12] She sees Jupiter Hammon as the first of a long line of neglected Negro authors, and she calls upon all teachers to inform their students about the contributions of black authors to American literature. This point of view is now becoming accepted, and many high schools and colleges offer special courses or programs in the area of black studies as well.

While the body of writings about Jupiter Hammon is small, there is a present awareness of the earlier neglect of Negro authors and a corresponding increase in the amount of material being written about them. This current attempt to place the Negro as a contributor to history and literature and not as a by-product of it will undoubtedly have a salutary effect on the writings of Jupiter Hammon and will help to establish his honored place in American literature.

The Wegelin study printed here is owned by the Huntington Public Library in Huntington, Long Island, where the Editor is Library Director.

A Winter Piece is a copy of the original in the Library of the Connecticut Historical Society in Hartford, Connecticut. Wegelin may not have seen this copy when he noted that "nothing in the chirography of Hammon has been found," for it is inscribed in a clear and bold hand: "For The Rev'd William Lockwood, from His firend (sic) & humble Serv't, The Author." (The Rev. William Lockwood (1753-1828) was a Connecticut minister, installed as pastor of the First Church of Glastonbury, Connecticut, in 1797.)

An Evening's Improvement was obtained from the copy in the New York Historical Society in New York City.

An Address to the Negroes in the State of New York, 1806 edition, which includes the testimonial to Hammon but is otherwise the same as earlier editions, was obtained from the copy in the Hanley Collection of the Smithtown Library of Smithtown, Long Island.

Feeling that the variations in spelling used by Jupiter Hammon and the printer give the work more flavor and authenticity, I have corrected the misspellings in only three or four instances, and then solely to avoid confusion.

The Editor appreciates the courtesy and the assistance of these institutions and their staff.

S.A.R.

Huntington, N.Y.
November, 1969

NOTES

1. Hammon states, " ...I am advanced to the age of seventy-one years..." on p. 20 of *An Evening's Improvement*, advertised as "just published" in the *Connecticut Courant*, March 4, 1783.
2. *International Library of Negro Life and History*. (Vol. 1) Historical Negro Biographies. N.Y., Publishers Co., Inc., 1967. p. 21.
3. Vertanes, Charles A. Jupiter Hammon; Early Negro Poet of L.I. In *Nassau County Historical Journal*, Vol. XVIII, No. 1, Winter, 1957. p. 4.
4. Hughes, Langston. *Poetry of the Negro*. Garden City, Doubleday, 1949.
5. Vertanes, op. cit., p. 6.
6. Ibid, p. 5.
7. Perkins, Nathan. *A Sermon Occasioned by the Unhappy Death of Mr. Lloyd; a refuge from Long Island*. June 18, 1780. Hartford, Hudson & Goodwin, 1780. A copy of this 19 page pamphlet is in the Library of the Connecticut Historical Society.
8. Overton, Jacqueline. *Long Island's Story*. 2nd ed. Port Washington, N.Y., Ira J. Friedman, Inc., 1961. p. 147.
9. Brawley, Benjamin. *Early Negro American Writers*. Freeport, N.Y., Books for Libraries Press, 1935 (Reprinted 1968). pp. 21-30.
10. Loggins, Vernon. *The Negro Author. His Development in America to 1900*. Port Washington, N.Y., Kennikat Press 1964, c1959.
11. McManus, Edgar J. *A History of Negro Slavery in New York*. Syracuse N.Y., Syracuse University Press, c1966.
12. Reese, Carolyn. "From Jupiter Hammon to LeRoi Jones." In *Changing Education*. Vol. 1, No. 3, Fall, 1966. p. 30-34 ff.

BIOGRAPHICAL SKETCH OF
JUPITER HAMMON
by Oscar Wegelin

"My old negroes are to be provided for." With these words ends the codicil to the will of Henry Lloyd, owner and lord of Lloyd's Neck, or Queen's Village, dated March 3, 1763.

While these words convey nothing of especial interest in themselves, they are to the student of American literature of paramount importance as among the "old Negroes" was a man, a slave, who was destined to become, nay, had already become the first one of his race to see his name in print as a writer of verse in what we are now pleased to call the United States of America.

For without doubt, Jupiter Hammon, the subject of this volume, was the first member of the Negro race to write and publish poetry in this country. For more than a century Phillis Wheatley has been lauded throughout the English-speaking world as the first of her race to appear in print as a versifier, at least so far as America was concerned. It will be shown however in this sketch of Hammon that not only did he antedate Miss Wheatley by nearly ten years as a poet, but at least one of his poems was printed before she had reached these shores, or knew one word of English.

The earliest trace of Hammon is found in a letter dated 1730 when the poet must have been a child of ten or twelve years. I give it in full, as follows:

"St. Georges May 19 1730

Sir: I'm informed by Mr Lloyd Jupiter is afflicted w [th]

21

pains in his Leggs Knees and thighs ascending to his
bowels wch in my Esteem is a gouty Rumatick Disorder to
releave which and Prevent the Impending Danger (as you
observe) of its getting up to his Stomach, Desire the
following Directions may be vsed. In the first place give
one of the Purges, In the morning fasting, and all night
one of the boluses, the next day take away about 12 or
14 ounces of blood (notwithstanding he loost blood in the
winter) from the foot will be the most serviceable a day
or two after as you find his strength will bear it, give the
other purge, and the bolus att night, on those days he
doth not purge and is bled give one of the powdrs in the
Morning and another in the Evening mixt in some Diet
Drink made of the equal of Horse Reddish Roots the
bark of elder Root Pine Budds or the second bark wood
or Toad sorrel, make it stronger with the Ingredients and
Lett him drink constantly of it for a month or six weeks
and then the remainder of the summer let him have milch
whey to drink he must live on a thin spare diet abstaining
from meat att nights all spiritous liquors salt pepper and
vinegar have sent home oyntmt to be used as he did the
former

with my affectionate Regard [s]
to Vncle and Aunt best Respects to all yr good family
I Remain
                Your Most Humble and Obed [t] serv [t]
                        G. Muirson."

Nearly twenty years ago the late Daniel Parish, Jr., told
the writer that he had in his collection a broadside poem
written by Hammon which was earlier than anything that
had been written by a Negro in America, as far as could be
traced. He had, however, mislaid it and could not recall its
title. As his statement seemed so remarkable, I at first
doubted its correctness, but as this gentleman was well
known as an expert among students of early American
poetry, I still hoped that what he said would some day be
proven. Until his death, which occurred in December of last
year, Mr. Parish was unable to find this elusive broadside,
and it seemed that it must be forever lost and the point that
I had tried to prove would be forever unsolved. Whenever
this "supposed" broadside was mentioned to any of the

delvers into the literature of the Colonial period, my sur-
mises regarding Hammon's priority as a poet were received
with grave doubt.

I, however, had faith in the statement made by the de-
parted collector and when a few months ago Mr. Chas.
Fred. Heartman issued his admirable bibliography of Miss
Wheatley, I determined to endeavor once more to locate the
long lost broadsheet. With this end in view I wrote to Mr.
Robert H. Kelby, Librarian of the New York Historical
Society, and inquired of that gentleman if perchance he had
discovered among a collection of pamphlets relating to slavery
which Mr. Parish had, prior to his death, presented to the
society, a broadside poem by one Jupiter Hammon. I de-
scribed the piece as well as I knew how, expecting that a
search would have to be made among a large lot of mater-
ial. Imagine my surprise when almost immediately I received
a reply stating that the broadside that I had been searching
for for years was not in the lot of pamphlets presented by
Mr. Parish, but was in its proper place among the broad-
sides belonging to the Society's collection, where it had evi-
dently been for many years.

This was certainly good news, as it proved peradventure
that my surmise had been correct, and that Miss Wheatley
would have to step down from the pedestal she had so long
occupied.

My ambition, however, in making this discovery was not
to dethrone the dusky versifier of Boston, but I wanted to
do justice to one who almost unknown, yet must have been
a man of considerable ability and of influence among the
members of his own race, bondman though he had been.

Unfortunately, none of his contemporaries seemed to have
left behind anything which would throw any light upon his
life, in fact the only thing that is known of this interesting
character is gathered from his own statements that appear in
the most popular of his writings, *An Address to the Negroes*

of the State of New York. In this address, which exhorts the slaves to be true to their masters, he writes, "When I was in Hartford in Connecticut, where I lived during the War, I published several pieces which were well received, not only by those of my own colour, but my a number of the White people, who thought they might do good among their servants. This is one consideration, among others, that emboldens me now to publish what I have written to you.... I am now upwards of seventy years old." This would make the date of his birth about 1720. Where he first saw the light of day, I am unable to state, in fact, were his birth place in Africa, or more probable, the West Indies, he himself was without doubt unable to give the exact date of his natal day. (The letter of Muirson seems to prove that he was born in this country.)

From the tenor of his writings, both poetical and prose, I am inclined to believe with Mr. A. A. Schomburg, that Hammon was a preacher among his people. Mr. Schomburg is almost certain that he preached or led religious gatherings, in Hartford and New Haven. His presence in Hartford during the period of the Revolutionary War is explained by the fact that his master, Joseph Lloyd, was a patriot and was compelled to forsake Long Island when the British and Hessians overran it.

The poem which establishes Hammon's priority as an American Negro versifier, is entitled, "An Evening Thought. Salvation by Christ, with Penentential Cries: Composed by Jupiter Hammon, a Negro belonging to Mr. Lloyd, of Queen's Village, on Long Island, the 25th of December, 1760." It is a broadside, evidently printed at New York early in the following year. The poem comprises 88 lines printed in double column.

Hammon was evidently much interested in Salvation as that word appears no less than twenty-three times in this poem. This slave served no less than three members of the

Lloyd family. At the time that this poem was written he was owned by Henry Lloyd, whom he served until the latter's death, which occurred in 1763. (I have mentioned the clause in his will which directed that his Negroes should be cared for.) At his death he left the Neck to his four sons, but Hammon became the property of Joseph, who when the British overran the Island fled to Connecticut. Joseph died during the War and left his part of the Neck to John Lloyd, Jr. This John, who was a grandson of Joseph, became the last owner of Hammon, who at this time was a man of about 60 years of age.

His second publication was a poetical address to Phillis Wheatley, dated "Hartford, August 4, 1778." It is also printed in broadsheet form, and only one copy is known to exist.

His next appearance in print was entitled, "An essay on the Ten Virgins." This was issued at Hartford the following year. I have been unable to locate a copy, but it was advertised as "To be sold" in *The Connecticut Courant*, Dec. 14, 1779.

Nothing now appeared from his pen until 1782, when Hudson & Goodwin printed at Hartford, "A Winter Piece." This was largely in prose, but contained on the last two pages, "A Poem for Children with thoughts on Death."

Hammon was evidently much taken up with thoughts on death, and in his "Address to the Negroes" he writes, "If we should ever get to Heaven, we shall find nobody to reproach us for being black, or for being slaves." Why the if?

His next appearance in print was a religious dissertation which he called "An Evening's Improvement." It was printed at Hartford, probably by Hudson & Goodwin, without date, but undoubtedly during the War. It contains a poetical dialogue, entitled, "The Kind Master and Dutiful Servant."

Hammon's masters were evidently kind to him, probably realizing that he was a slave of more than usual intelligence.

As will be seen by referring to the list of his writings at the
end of this volume, his friends, among whom were un-
doubtedly some of the members of the Lloyd family, were
of assistance to the author in bringing his writings before
the public. Without this help, it is doubtful if any of his
writings should have seen the light of day, as Hammon was
not well enough known to have publishers as anxious to
print his writings, as they were, to issue the poems of Phillis
Wheatley. While the latter's writings have been issued in
many editions, not only in America, but in Europe as well,
those of the Long Island slave never reached beyond a single
edition, with the exception of the "Address to the Negroes,"
of which as many as three editions were printed, one after
the writer's decease.

Hammon's most important work, probably his last, was
not in verse, but was an Address to the Negroes of the state
in which he dwelt. Its influence was, however, felt beyond
the borders of New York, and we find an edition printed in
Philadelphia by Daniel Humphreys the year in which the
first made its appearance from the press of Carroll and
Patterson. This was in 1787. An edition was also printed in
New York, 1806, after the author had ceased to be a slave,
and (let us hope) had found rest for his soul in that Heaven
he had longed for so often and about which he had written
his best lines.

A receipt for money which mentions Hammon is in the
New York Historical Society and proves that he was living
as late as 1790. I herewith give a copy of it.

"Oysterbay 6th Oct 1790 Recd of John Lloyd Junr
twelve Pound in full of the last years Interest on his bond
Recd by the hand of Jupiter Hammon & have endorsed it
on the Bond

                                   P   Loretta Cock"
      £12-0-0

The year of his death is unknown, but it was between the

years 1790 and 1806. In the edition of the Address to the Negroes issued in 1806 three residents of Oyster Bay, Long Island, attest over their own signatures that Hammon was a man of good parts and an esteemed neighbor. The publishers of the 1787 edition state that "They have made no material alterations in it, except in the spelling, which they found needed considerable correction." By this it will be seen that Hammon was evidently a man without education. How different a career compared with that of Miss Wheatley, who had the advantages of a good schooling. He, a slave faithfully serving both his Heavenly and earthly Masters, probably almost unknown outside of a small circle in which he moved, while she the child of fortune was petted by all with whom she came in contact. Only an accident prevented her from being introduced to the King of England, George the Third, and the father of his country honored her by sending her an autograph letter.

A few years later, however, she died, broken in spirit, and almost friendless, her later days being darkened through an unfortunate marriage. Her husband, although a man of talent, could not appreciate the gentle and kindly being he had sworn to protect. The portrait affixed to the first edition of her poems shows a face marked with kindness and trust in others. What would we not give to obtain a likeness of "The Negro Servant of John Lloyd, Jr., of Queen's Village."

Several specimens of the hand-writing of Miss Wheatley are known to exist, but nothing in the chirography of Hammon has been found. Were it not for his printed pamphlets and broadsides his very name would now be forgotten and the first of his race to write verse in America would have none to do him honor. Hammon was, however, the earliest Negro versifier and a not unworthy forerunner of a numerous company of Afro-American poets, the best of whom was the lamented Paul Laurence Dunbar.

In two respects both Hammon and Miss Wheatley were

alike. They were both of a deeply religious temperament, and both tried to instill their belief into others. How far they succeeded is not for us to decide, but it seems probable that the exhortations of Hammon to his fellow slaves did meet with success. At any rate his white neighbors seemed pleased with his efforts and did what they could to help him.

Although Hammon must have been well known to some of his contemporaries, he is almost totally neglected by biographers and bibliographers. Nor is he mentioned in any of the histories of Long Island. The only notices I have found regarding him, beyond the mere mention of his name, are the following:

"Jupiter Hammon, a Negro Slave of Long Island, attained to considerable advancement, both in an intellectual and religious point of view. He published an address to the Negroes of New York, which contains much excellent advice, embodied in language so excellent, that were it not well attested, its genuiness might be justly questioned." Armisted. "*A Tribute to the Negro,*" Manchester, 1848.

"Joseph (Lloyd) had a Negro slave, Jupiter Hammon, who was quite a literary character, and published at Hartford, Dec. '79 an Essay on the Parable of the Ten Virgins." Onderdonk. *Revolutionary Incidents of Queens County.*

The present writer contributed an article on Hammon in the *Literary Collector* for August, 1904. It was headed, "Was Phillis Wheatley America's First Negro Poet?"

Several books relating to the Lloyd Family have been published, one at least by a member of the Family, but not even the name of the slave-poet is mentioned in either of them. Fate seemed anxious to consign him to oblivion, but thanks to the indefatigable searcher for books who first called my attention to the fact that such a man once lived, I am now enabled to place these facts, meagre though they be, before the public. It seems probable that Hammon was the author of more poetry than has been unearthed, but after a diligent search through many of the important public and private libraries of the United States those noted in the bibliography at the end of this volume are all that could be discovered. If there were more, they, like "An Evening Thought" and "An Address to Phillis Wheatley," were probably issued in broadsheet form and have long since vanished. Happily, however, the broadside which furnishes proof of his priority as a poet of colour exists in the single copy now in the New York Historical Society.

In the bibliography I have noted the whereabouts of copies that could be located. In the gathering of the material which made this book possible, imperfect though it may be, I have received valuable assistance from the librarians of the New York Historical Society, the American Antiquarian Society, the John Carter Brown Library, the Massachusetts Historical Society, the New York Public Library, the Long Island Historical Society, the Boston Public Library, and Harvard College Library. Especially am I grateful for assistance rendered by Messrs. Robert H. Kelby, Librarian of the New York Historical Society; Albert C. Bates, Librarian of the Connecticut Historical Society; Orville B. Ackerly, who furnished me with the copy of the Lloyd will of 1763, and Mr. Arthur A. Schomburg, who spent much time in seeking information in some of the libraries of the Nutmeg State.

HAMMON AS A POET

As a poet Hammon will certainly not rank among the "Immortals." His verse is stilted, and while some of his rhymings are fairly even, we can easily comprehend that they were written by one not well versed in the art of poesy. They have a sameness which is wearying to the reader and there is too much reiteration, in some cases the same or nearly the same words being employed again and again.

His verse is saturated with a religious feeling not always well expressed, as he did not possess the ability to use the right word at the proper time. Hammon was undoubtedly deeply religious, but his religion was somewhat tinged with narrowness and superstition, a not uncommon fault of the time in which he lived and wrote.

Although grammatically almost perfect, it seems certain that an abler and more experienced hand than his own was responsible for this.

Compared with the verses of Phillis Wheatley, his lines are commonplace and few would care to read them more than once. When we consider, however, that this poor slave had probably no other learning than what he had been enabled to secure for himself during his hours of relaxation from labor, it is surprising that the results are not more meagre. Although his rhymings can hardly be dignified by the name of poetry, they are certainly not inferior to many of the rhymings of his day and generation.

As before noted, his lines breathe a deep religious feeling and were written with the hope that those who would read them would be led from the ways of sin to righteousness. His poetical address to Miss Wheatley was written with this end in view and may have had more than a passing effect on that young woman.

He was found of using certain words, and "Salvation" was one of his favorites, it being made use of twenty-three times in his earliest known publication. In this respect he was not unlike the late Bloodgood Cutter, whose favorite word was "did." As a rhymer, however, Hammon far out-shines the "Long Island Farmer Poet," who used to boast of his lack of education.

Hammon was also fond of using marginal references from Scripture and in some of his writings they are found at every second line. He was evidently a deep student of the Bible and was inspired by what the Good Book taught him. It seems probable that his effusions were the means of bringing many of his fellow bondmen to the throne of grace.

When we consider that he was probably without any education whatsoever, we marvel that he accomplished as much as he did. Had he had the advantages of learning possessed by Miss Wheatley, it seems possible that as a poet he would have ranked as her equal, if not her superior. His prose writings were also above the mediocre, but from the testimony of one of his printers he was evidently deficient as a speller.

He stands, however, unique in the annals of American poetry and his works must not be too harshly judged. The disadvantages under which he composed them were probably far greater than we can imagine.

It seems, however, too bad that his verse is entirely of a religious nature. Much would have been added to its interest had he written about some of the events that were transpiring all around him during the War for Independence and the years that followed that struggle.

He seems to have been content to sing the praises of the Master whom he longed to serve and whose reward he some day expected to receive, and with that end in view he labored to instill the blessings of religion into his less fortunate brethren.

For this his memory should be honored and let the broken lines which fell from his pen be cherished, if for no other reason than that they were written by the first American Negro who attempted to give expression to his thoughts in verse.

A VISIT TO HAMMON'S HOME

On the invitation of Mr. Orville B. Ackerly, the best informed student of Long Island history, that gentleman, Mrs.

Ackerly and myself motored to Lloyd's Neck on the morning of October 17, last. We were in quest of the last resting place of the poet. Did we find it? No, but the trip was one of the most enjoyable that I have undertaken.

After driving some thirty miles after leaving Jamaica, we arrived at the "Neck," and stopped at the old Lloyd Manor House, now owned by Wm. J. Matheson, and occupied by his daughter, Mrs. W. D. Wood, where we hoped to obtain some information regarding Hammon's grave. The lady, however, was not at home, but one of her employees directed us to the home of one Meyer, a German, who had a reputation of being an authority on the early history of the "Neck." We found him, but as I had expected, he knew nothing about Hammon, but he informed us that the old Lloyd burial plot was no more and that the remains of those interred there had been removed to the Rural Cemetary at Huntington. His daughter, however, directed us to a small burial plot situated in the midst of a dense wood and told us that was where she believed the grave of Hammon might be found. After some search and after wending our way over a path well nigh obliterated with weeds and underbrush, we espied in a little inclosure a few headstones. How my heart beat high with expectation! At last I was to look upon the last resting place of the old slave-poet. Perhaps the dates of his birth and death were graven thereon; an extract from his poems might even be found cut into the stone?

But no, we are doomed to disappointment, for the plot we had found was the "God's Acre" of some of the tenants of Mr. Lloyd. The earliest death noted was that of Thomas Barker who died in 1795 AE. 81.

Mr. Ackerly, who carried his note book with him, made a copy of the inscriptions found on the headstones in the plot, but like myself he is of the opinion that Hammon's remains did not repose there. On our return we stopped once more at the Meyer home, but the old German could not be discovered and a notice on his door informed us that he was "out in the woods."

The site of the Lloyd graveyard is now occupied by a neat school house.

Though our trip was without tangible results, it was not altogether useless and I was certainly glad to gaze on the scenes once familiar to the subject of this book, and to ramble through the woods where he was wont to roam, perhaps sitting beneath the shade of some monarch of the forest, mayhap composing beneath the overhanging leaves some of the verses which are to-day his chief claim to fame.

HAMMON'S VIEWS ON SLAVERY

Hammon's "An Address to the Negroes of the State of New York" shows plainly that Hammon did not regard slavery as lawful according to the laws of the Creator. He, however, believed it better for his colored brethren to meekly obey their earthly masters as by doing so their condition would be bettered and the hearts of their owners softened thereby. From his own statements he was a favored servant and his life was evidently one of comparative ease. He himself was perfectly content to remain in bondage, but longed to see the younger Negroes freed.

That his advice was deemed of value is proved by the fact that the Pennsylvania Society for Promoting the Abolition of Slavery ordered the book to be reprinted in an edition of five hundred copies. His plea for the liberation of the younger Negroes seems to have had an effect on his owner for in his will dated 1795 John Lloyd, Jr., directs that certain of his Negroes, whom he names, should be given their freedom on reaching the age of twenty-eight.

CRITICAL ANALYSIS OF THE WORKS OF JUPITER HAMMON

by
Vernon Loggins

Probably the first poem published by an American Negro is a broadside of eighty-eight lines entitled *An Evening Thought: Salvation by Christ with Penetential Cries: Composed by Jupiter Hammon, a Negro Belonging to Mr. Lloyd, of Queen's Village, on Long Island, the 25th of December, 1760.* Little is known of Jupiter Hammon. Born about 1720, he lived through the years when the church in America was being democratized, through the period when the Revolution was remaking the thought of the country, and on until the definite establishment of the United States as a nation. All of his life he passed in slavery, belonging, as title-pages of his publications attest, to three different members of the Lloyd family of Long Island. Except for the time during the War of the Revolution when the British were in possession of Long Island and the patriot Lloyds with their slaves were in exile in Hartford, Connecticut, Jupiter Hammon's residence was probably on the Lloyd estate near Queen's Village. Aside from his own statement that he was "able to do almost any kind of business," there seem to be no records giving information regarding his exact status as a slave; and we do not know whether he was a farm laborer, a household servant, or a workman at some trade.

The Lloyds were evidently humane and considerate masters; for Hammon, addressing his fellow slaves, wrote in 1786:

> I have good reason to be thankful that my lot is so much better than most slaves have had. I suppose I have had more advantages than most of you who are slaves have ever known, and I believe more than many white people have enjoyed.

Whatever advantages and privileges the Lloyds might have granted him, there is no indication in his writings that they gave him opportunity for instruction beyond the most elementary training in reading and writing. But they undoubtedly allowed him to go freely to church, where he absorbed the doctrines of the Calvinistic Methodists, of which all of his work is an echo. His masters also, it seems, left him free at times to engage in preaching. Stimulated by religious indulgences, he read with avidity the Bible and hymn books and possibly such pious poems as Michael Wigglesworth's *The Day of Doom*. It was in all probability through this reading that he taught himself what he knew about prose style and the art of versification.

Hammon said in 1786: "When I was at Hartford, in Connecticut, where I lived during the war, I published several pieces which were well received, not only by those of my own colour, but by a number of the white people, who thought they might do good among the servants." *An Address to Miss Phillis Wheatly,* a poem of twenty-one ballad stanzas, appeared as a broadside in 1778. In 1779, came *An Essay on the Ten Virgins,* of which no copy seems to exist. That it was published, however, is scarcely to be doubted, since it was advertised in the *Connecticut Courant* for December 14, 1779. *A Winter Piece,* a sermon in prose with "A Poem for Children with Thoughts on Death" tacked on at the end, appeared in pamphlet form in 1782. Another prose pamphlet, *An Evening's Improvement,* including also a dialogue in verse entitled "The Kind Master and the Dutiful Servant," was published at Hartford without date. These four pieces written during the Revolution, with *An Evening Thought* (1760) and *An Address to the Negroes of the State of New-York* (1787), make up all of the known writings of Jupiter Hammon. That he produced other broadsides and pamphlets of which there is at present no apparent trace is altogether possible.

It is an interesting coincidence that most of Hammon's poetry was published at Hartford at a time when that Connecticut town was the literary capital of America. But if the neoclassical "Hartford Wits" read his poems, they no doubt looked upon them as chaotic effusions of crude thoughts poured out in a verse not inappropriate to the cheapest balladry. To the twentieth-century mind, which places a high value on the artlessness of folk poetry, Jupiter Hammon's work takes on a new meaning. There is a strength of wild and native religious feeling in what he wrote, a strength which he achieved without conscious effot. From hearing evangelical sermons and from reading the Bible according to his own untrained fancy, he picked up strange notions regarding salvation, penitential cries, redeeming love, tribunal day, the Holy Word, bounteous mercies. His mystic Negro mind played with these notions; and, endowed with the instinct for music which is so strong in his race, he sang out his impressions in such meters as he had become familiar with in the hymns of Charles Wesley and Augustus Montague Toplady, and in such rimes as for the moment pleased his ear. Indeed, his method of composition must have been that of the unknown makers of the spirituals.

Like the spirituals, the poems of Jupiter Hammon were composed to be heard. There is evident in his verse that peculiar sense for sound which is the most distinguishing characteristic of Negro folk poetry. A word that appeals to his ear he uses over and over again, in order, it seems, to cast a spell with it. In *An Evening Thought* the word *salvation* occurs in every three or four lines. Any impressionable sinners who might have heard Jupiter Hammon chant the poem when in the ecstasy of religious emotion no doubt went away to be haunted by the sound of the word *salvation* if not by the idea. A few lines will illustrate the effectiveness of the repetition:

> Salvation comes now from the Lord,
> Our victorious King.
> His holy name be well ador'd,
> Salvation surely bring.
> Dear Jesus give thy spirit now,
> Thy grace to every Nation,
> That han't the Lord to whom we bow,
> The author of Salvation.
> Dear Jesus, unto Thee we cry,
> Give us the preparation;
> Turn not away thy tender eye;
> We seek thy true Salvation.

In the original broadside the poem was printed, as here quoted, without a break between stanzas; however, the metrical arrangement is that of the ballad stanza with alternating rimes, a verse form which is often found in the early Methodist hymns, and which is the basis for the stanza in Wigglesworth's *The Day of Doom.* Hammon followed this pattern in all of his poems, though not without marked irregularities. There are numerous cases of wrenched accents demanding an outrageous pronunciation. There are many examples of syncopation, so characteristic of Negro dance rhythms, evident in the omission at times of one syllable and at other times of two, as in the following line, which is supposed to be tetrameter:

> Thou mightst   been left behind.

But the most interesting irregularities are the strange rime combinations—such as *word* and *God, Lord* and *God, call*

and *soul, sound* and *down.* Since we know little about how
English was spoken by the Negroes on Long Island in the
eighteenth century, we cannot determine how far astray
Jupiter Hammon's ear was in hearing exact rimes in such
combinations. We can say with definiteness that the riming
words which he selected are always sonorous.

While the imagery in Hammon's poems is in general re-
strained, often taken bodily from the New Testament, there
are unexpected turns in the thought which suggest the wild
extravagance of the spiritual. The unusual association of
ideas in the following stanza from *An Address to Miss Phillis
Wheatly* is probably the result of a necessity for rimes:

> God's tender mercy brought thee here;
> Tost o'er the raging main;
> In Christian faith thou hast a share,
> Worth all the gold of Spain.

The last three lines of the following stanza from the same
poem might not seem out of place in a spiritual:

> That thou a pattern still might be,
> To youth of Boston town,
> The blessed Jesus set thee free
> From every sinful wound.

In two stanzas of "A Poem for Children with Thoughts on
Death" Hammon pictures the dread terror of the day of
final judgment. Back of the ominous words of warning to
sinful children there is a delightful feeling of playfulness,
suggestive of a traditional Southern mammy threatening a
wilful infant with the imminent approach of a voodoo man.

> Then shall ye hear the trumpet sound,
> The graves give up their dead,
> Those blessed saints shall quick awake,
> And leave their dusty beds.
>
> Then shall ye hear the trumpet sound,
> And rend the native sky,

> Those bodies starting from the ground,
> In the twinkling of an eye.

In "The Kind Master and the Dutiful Servant," written in
dialogue, a form which indicates that the author might have
known something of the English popular ballad, Hammon
suddenly leaves the drama six stanzas from the end and
naïvely addresses his readers in his own person.

> Believe me now, my Christian friends,
> Believe your friend call'd Hammon:
> You cannot to your God attend,
> And serve the God of Mammon.

It must not be supposed that Jupiter Hammon was only
primitive and naïve, merely a folk poet incapable of consis-
tent and orderly reflection. *An Address to Miss Phillis
Wheatly,* his second poem, written eighteen years after his
first spontaneous and chaotic effort, *An Evening Thought,*
shows a balanced structure of ideas, based on the theme
that it was a divine providence which brought Phillis Wheat-
ley from heathen Africa to a land where she could know the
true religion and teach it to others. Both this poem and
"A Poem for Children with Thoughts on Death" are pro-
vided with scriptural glosses, and in each the thought asso-
ciation with the Biblical citations is fairly logical and exact.
While the two earlier prose pamphlets, *A Winter Piece* and
An Evening's Improvement, intended as sermons, are rhap-
sodic and incoherent, the *Address to the Negroes in the
State of New-York* displays a regular and firm organization.
It opens with personal reminiscences, and these are followed
by a series of moral precepts. Negroes are admonished to be
obedient and faithful to their masters, to be honest and not
to steal, to be energetic and not to dally when sent on er-
rands, to be always religious and never profane. In the
closing section, which deals with the subject of freedom for
the slaves, Hammon praises the blessings of liberty. But

concerning his own condition of slavery he mildly concludes:

> Now I acknowledge that liberty is a great thing, and
> worth seeking for, if we can get it honestly; and by our
> good conduct prevail on our masters to set us free: though
> for my own part I do not wish to be free; for many of us
> who are grown up slaves, and have always had masters
> to take care of us, should hardly know how to take care
> of themselves; and it may be for our own comfort to
> remain as we are.

Perhaps because of this concilatory attitude toward slavery,
Jupiter Hammon's work was disregarded by the early Negro
leaders, who in most cases kept alive the personalities of
their predecessors of any distinction whatsoever. The name
of America's first Negro poet dropped into oblivion soon
after his death, to remain there for more than a century.
His attempts at thoughtful composition, such as *An Address
to the Negroes in the State of New-York,* fall low in the
class of the subliterary. It is his poetry, with all of its art-
lessness and crudeness, which makes his name important. As
the product of the uncultivated Negro imagination and tem-
perament, his verse, slight as the body of it is, forms a
unique contribution to American poetry in the eighteenth
century. The reader of today is likely to find a more sincere
feeling in it than in most religious verse written in America
during Hammon's age. It is a quaint prelude to the rich and
varied songs which were to burst spontaneously from the
Negro folk a little later, songs which make up the great gift
from Africa to the art of America.

The Poetry of Jupiter Hammon

AN
Evening THOUGHT.

SALVATION BY *CHRIST*,
WITH
PENETENTIAL CRIES:

Composed by Jupiter Hammon, a Negro belonging to Mr Lloyd, of Queen's-
Village, on Long-Island, the 25th of December, 1760.

SALVATION comes by Jesus Christ alone,
 The only Son of God;
Redemption now to every one,
 That love his holy Word.
Dear Jesus we would fly to Thee,
 And leave off every Sin,
Thy tender Mercy well agree;
 Salvation from our King.
Salvation comes now from the Lord,
 Our victorious King;
His holy Name be well ador'd,
 Salvation surely bring.
Dear Jesus give thy Spirit now,
 Thy Grace to every Nation,
That han't the Lord to whom we bow,
 The Author of Salvation.
Dear Jesus unto Thee we cry,
 Give us thy Preparation;
Turn not away thy tender Eye;
 We seek thy true Salvation.
Salvation comes from God we know,
 The true and only One;
It's well agreed and certain true,
 He gave his only Son.
Lord hear our penetential Cry:
 Salvation from above;
It is the Lord that doth supply,
 With his Redeeming Love.
Dear Jesus by thy precious Blood,
 The World Redemption have:
Salvation comes now from the Lord,
 He being thy captive Slave.
Dear Jesus let the Nations cry,
 And all the People say,
Salvation comes from Christ on high,
 Haste on Tribunal Day.
We cry as Sinners to the Lord,
 Salvation to obtain;
It is firmly fixt his holy Word,
 Ye shall not cry in vain.
Dear Jesus unto Thee we cry,
 And make our Lamentation:
O let our Prayers ascend on high;
 We felt thy Salvation.

Lord turn our dark benighted Souls;
 Give us a true Motion,
And let the Hearts of all the World,
 Make Christ their Salvation.
Ten Thousand Angels cry to Thee,
 Yea louder than the Ocean.
Thou art the Lord, we plainly see;
 Thou art the true Salvation.
Now is the Day, excepted Time;
 The Day of Salvation;
Increase your Faith, do not repine:
 Awake ye every Nation.
Lord unto whom now shall we go,
 Or seek a safe Abode;
Thou hast the Word Salvation too
 The only Son of God.
Ho! every one that hunger hath,
 Or pineth after me,
Salvation be thy leading Staff,
 To set the Sinner free.
Dear Jesus unto Thee we fly;
 Depart, depart from Sin,
Salvation doth at length supply,
 The Glory of our King.
Come ye Blessed of the Lord,
 Salvation gently given;
O turn your Hearts, accept the Word,
 Your Souls are fit for Heaven.
Dear Jesus we now turn to Thee,
 Salvation to obtain;
Our Hearts and Souls do meet again,
 To magnify thy Name.
Come holy Spirit, Heavenly Dove,
 The Object of our Care;
Salvation doth increase our Love;
 Our Hearts hath felt thy fear.
Now Glory be to God on High,
 Salvation high and low;
And thus the Soul on Christ rely,
 To Heaven surely go.
Come Blessed Jesus, Heavenly Dove,
 Accept Repentance here;
Salvation give, with tender Love;
 Let us with Angels share.

F I N I S.

AN EVENING THOUGHT
SALVATION BY CHRIST, WITH PENETENTIAL CRIES

Salvation comes by Jesus Christ alone,
    The only Son of God;
Redemption now to every one,
    That love his holy Word.
Dear Jesus we would fly to Thee,
    And leave off every Sin,
Thy tender Mercy well agree;
    Salvation from our King.
Salvation comes now from the Lord,
    Our victorious King;
His holy Name be well ador'd,
    Salvation surely bring.
Dear Jesus give they Spirit now,
    Thy Grace to every Nation,
That han't the Lord to whom we bow,
    The Author of Salvation.
Dear Jesus unto Thee we cry,
    Give us the Preparation;
Turn not away thy tender Eye;
    We seek thy true Salvation.
Salvation comes from God we know,
    The true and only One;
It's well agreed and certain true,
    He gave his only Son.
Lord hear our penetential Cry:
    Salvation from above;
It is the Lord that doth supply,
    With his Redeeming Love.
Dear Jesus by thy precious Blood,
    The World Redemption have:

Salvation now comes from the Lord,
  He being thy captive slave.
Dear Jesus let the Nations cry,
  And all the People say,
Salvation comes from Christ on high,
  Haste on Tribunal Day.
We cry as Sinners to the Lord,
  Salvation to obtain;
It is firmly fixt his holy Word,
  Ye shall not cry in vain.
Dear Jesus unto Thee we cry,
  And make our Lamentation:
O let our Prayers ascend on high;
  We felt thy Salvation.
Lord turn our dark benighted Souls;
  Give us a true Motion,
And let the Hearts of all the World,
  Make Christ their Salvation.
Ten Thousand Angels cry to Thee,
  Yea louder than the Ocean.
Thou art the Lord, we plainly see;
  Thou art the true Salvation.
Now is the Day, excepted Time;
  The Day of Salvation;
Increase your Faith, do not repine:
  Awake ye every Nation.
Lord unto whom now shall we go,
  Or seek a safe Abode;
Thou hast the Word Salvation too
  The only Son of God.
Ho! every one that hunger hath,
  Or pineth after me,
Salvation be thy leading Staff,
  To set the Sinner free.
Dear Jesus unto Thee we fly;
  Depart, depart from Sin,
Salvation doth at length supply,
  The Glory of our King.
Come ye Blessed of the Lord,
  Salvation greatly given;
O turn your Hearts, accept the Word,
  Your Souls are fit for Heaven.

Dear Jesus we now turn to Thee,
  Salvation to obtain;
Our Hearts and Souls do meet again,
  To magnify thy Name.
Come holy Spirit, Heavenly Dove,
  The Object of our Care;
Salvation doth increase our Love;
  Our Hearts hath felt thy fear.
Now Glory be to God on High,
  Salvation high and low;
And thus the Soul on Christ rely,
  To Heaven surely go.
Come Blessed Jesus, Heavenly Dove,
  Accept Repentance here;
Salvation give, with tender Love;
  Let us with Angels share.

An ADDRESS to Miss PHILLIS WHEATLY, Ethiopian Poetess, in Boston, who came from Africa at eight years of age, and soon became acquainted with the Gospel of Jesus Christ.

Miss Wheatly; pray give me leave to express as follows:

1
O Come you pious youth! adore
  The wisdom of thy God,
In bringing thee from distant shore,
  To learn his holy word.   Eccles. xii.

2
Thou mightst been left behind,
  Amidst a dark abode;
God's tender mercy still combin'd,
  Thou hast the holy word.   Psal. cxxxv. 2, 3.

3
Fair Wisdom's ways are paths of peace,
  And they that walk therein,
Shall reap the joys that never cease,
  And Christ shall be their king.   Psal. i. 1, 2.
                                               Prov. iii. 7.

4
God's tender mercy brought thee here,
  Tost o'er the raging main;
In Christian faith thou hast a share,
  Worth all the gold of Spain.   Psal. ciii. 1, 3, 4.

5
While thousands toss'd by the sea,
  And others settled down,
God's tender mercy set thee free,
  From dangers still unknown.   Death.

6
That thou a pattern still might be,
  To youth of Boston town,
The blessed Jesus set thee free,
  From every sinful wound.   2 Cor. v. 10.

7
The blessed Jesus, who came down,
  Unvail'd his sacred face,
To cleanse the soul of every wound,
  And give repenting grace.   Rom. v. 21.

8
That we poor sinners may obtain
  The pardon of our sin;
Dear blessed Jesus now constrain,
  And bring us flocking in.   Psal. xxxiv. 6, 8.

9
Come you, Phillis, now aspire,
  And seek the living God,
So step by step thou mayst go higher,
  Till perfect in the word.   Matth. vii. 7, 8.

10
While thousands mov'd to distant shore,
  And others left behind,
The blessed Jesus still adore,
  Implant this in thy mind.   Psal. lxxxix. 1.

11
Thou hast left the heathen shore,
  Thro' mercy of the Lord;   Psal. xxxiv. 1, 2, 3.

12
Among the heathen live no more,
  Come magnify thy God.

13
I pray the living God may be,
  The shepherd of thy soul;
His tender mercies still are free,
  His mysteries to unfold.   Psal. lxxx. 1, 2, 3.

14
Thou, Phillis, when thou hunger hast,
  Or pantest for thy God;
Jesus Christ is thy relief,
  Thou hast the holy word.   Psal. xlii. 1, 2, 3.

15
The bounteous mercies of the Lord,
  Are hid beyond the sky,
And holy souls that love his word,
  Shall taste them when they die.   Psal. xvi. 10, 11.

16
These bounteous mercies are from God,
  The merit of his Son;
The humble soul that loves his word,
  He chooses for his own.   Psal. xxxiv. 15.

17
Come, dear Phillis, be advis'd,
  To drink Samaria's flood;   John iv. 13, 14.

18
But Christ's redeeming blood.

19
While thousands muse with earthly toys,
  And range about the street,
Dear Phillis, seek for heaven's joys,
  Where we do hope to meet.   Matth. vi. 33.

20
When God shall send his summons down,
  And number saints together,
Blest angels chant, (triumphant sound)
  Come live with me for ever.   Psal. cxvi. 15.

21
The humble soul shall fly to God,
  And leave the things of time,
Start forth as 'twere at the first word,
  To taste things more divine.   Mat. v. 3, 6.

22
Behold! the soul shall waft away,
  Whene'er we come to die,
And leave its cottage made of clay,
  In twinkling of an eye.   Cor. xv. 51, 52, 53.

23
Now glory be to the Most High,
  United praises given,
By all on earth, incessantly,
  And all the host of heav'n.   Psal. cl. 6.

Composed by JUPITER HAMMON, a Negro Man belonging to Mr. Joseph Lloyd, of Queen's Village, on Long-Island, now in Hartford.

The above lines are published by the Author, and a number of his friends, who desire to join with him in their best regards to Miss Wheatly.

AN ADDRESS
TO
MISS PHILLIS WHEATLY

I

O come you pious youth! adore
    The wisdom of thy God,
In bringing thee from distant shore,
    To learn His holy word.

                Eccles. xii.

II

Thou mightst been left behind
    Amidst a dark abode;
God's tender mercy still combin'd,
    Thou hast the holy word.

            Psal. cxxxv, 2, 3.

III

Fair wisdom's ways are paths of peace,
    And they that walk therein,
Shall reap the joys that never cease,
    And Christ shall be their king.

          Psal. i. 1, 2; Prov. iii, 7.

IV

God's tender mercy brought thee here;
    Tost o'er the raging main;
In Christian faith thou hast a share,
    Worth all the gold of Spain.

              Psal. ciii, 1, 3, 4,

49

V

While thousands tossed by the sea,
   And others settled down,
God's tender mercy set thee free,
   From dangers that come down.

Death.

VI

That thou a pattern still might be,
   To youth of Boston town,
The blessed Jesus set thee free,
   From every sinful wound.

2 Cor. v, 10.

VII

The blessed Jesus, who came down,
   Unvail'd his sacred face,
To cleanse the soul of every wound,
   And give repenting grace.

Rom. v, 21.

VIII

That we poor sinners may obtain,
   The pardon of our sin;
Dear blessed Jesus now constrain,
   And bring us flocking in.

Psal. xxxiv, 6, 7, 8.

IX

Come you, Phillis, now aspire,
   And seek the living God,
So step by step thou mayst go higher,
   Till perfect in the word.

Matth. vii, 7, 8.

X

While thousands mov'd to distant shore,
   And others left behind,
The blessed Jesus still adore,
   Implant this in thy mind.

Psal. lxxxix. 1.

XI

Thou hast left the heathen shore;
   Thro' mercy of the Lord,
Among the heathen live no more,
   Come magnify thy God.

Psal. xxxiv. 1, 2, 3.

XII

I pray the living God may be,
   The shepherd of thy soul;
His tender mercies still are free,
   His mysteries to unfold.

Psal. lxxx. 1, 2, 3.

XIII

Thou, Phillis, when thou hunger hast,
   Or pantest for thy God;
Jesus Christ is thy relief,
   Thou hast the holy word.

Psal. xiii. 1, 2, 3.

XIV

The bounteous mercies of the Lord,
   Are hid beyond the sky,
And holy souls that love His word,
   Shall taste them when they die.

Psal. xvi, 10, 11.

XV

These bounteous mercies are from God,
    The merits of His Son;
The humble soul that loves His word,
    He chooses for His own.

                                    Psal. xxxiv. 15.

XVI

Come, dear Phillis, be advis'd,
    To drink Samaria's flood;
There nothing that shall suffice
    But Christ's redeeming blood.

                                    John iv, 13, 14.

XVII

While thousands muse with earthly toys;
    And range about the street,
Dear Phillis, seek for heaven's joys,
    Where we do hope to meet.

                                    Matth. vi, 33.

XVIII

When God shall send his summons down,
    And number saints together,
Blest angels chant, (triumphant sound),
    Come live with me forever.

                                    Psal. cxvi, 15.

XIX

The humble soul shall fly to God,
    And leave the things of time,
Start forth as 'twere at the first word,
    To taste things more divine.

                                    Matth. v, 3, 8.

XX

Behold! the soul shall waft away,
   Whene'er we come to die,
And leave its cottage made of clay,
   In twinkling of an eye.

Cor. xv, 51, 52, 53

XXI

Now glory be to the Most High,
   United praises given,
By all on earth, incessantly,
   And all the host of heav'n.

Psal. cl, 6.

A POEM FOR CHILDREN WITH THOUGHTS
ON DEATH

I

O Ye young and thoughtless youth,
  Come seek the living God,
The scriptures are a sacred truth,
  Ye must believe the word.

Eccle. xii. 1.

II

Tis God alone can make you wise,
  His wisdom's from above,
He fills the soul with sweet supplies
  By his redeeming love.

Prov. iv. 7.

III

Remember youth the time is short,
  Improve the present day
And pray that God may guide your thoughts,
  and teach your lips to pray.

Psalm xxx. 9.

IV

To pray unto the most high God,
  and beg restraining grace,
Then by the power of his word
  You'l see the Saviour's face.

54

V

Little children they may die,
　　Turn to their native dust,
Their souls shall leap beyond the skies,
　　And live among the just.

VI

Like little worms they turn and crawl,
　　and gasp for every breath.
The blessed Jesus sends his call,
　　and takes them to his rest.

VII

Thus the youth are born to die,
　　The time is hastening on,
The Blessed Jesus rends the sky,
　　and makes his power known.

Psalm ciii. 15.

VIII

Then ye shall hear the angels sing
　　The trumpet give a sound,
Glory, glory to our King,
　　The Saviour's coming down.

Matth. xxvi. 64.

IX

Start ye saints from dusty beds,
　　and hear a Saviour call,
Twas Jesus Christ that died and bled,
　　and thus preserv'd thy soul.

X

This the portion of the just,
　Who lov'd to serve the Lord,
Their bodies starting from the dust,
　Shall rest upon their God.

XI

They shall join that holy word,
　That angels constant sing,
Glory, glory to the Lord,
　Hallelujahs to our King.

XII

Thus the Saviour will appear,
　With guards of heavenly host,
Those blessed Saints, shall then declare,
　Tis Father, Son and Holy Ghost.

Rev. i. 7, 8.

XIII

Then shall ye hear the trumpet sound,
　The graves give up their dead,
Those blessed saints shall quick awake,
　and leave their dusty beds.

Matth. xxvii. 51, 52.

XIV

Then shall you hear the trumpet sound,
　and rend the native sky,
Those bodies starting from the ground,
　In the twinkling of an eye.

I Cor. xv. 51, 52, 53, 54.

XV

There to sing the parise of God,
   and join the angelic train,
And by the power of his word,
   Unite together again.

XVI

Where angels stand for to admit
   Their souls at the first word,
Cast sceptres down at Jesus feet
   Crying holy holy Lord.

XVII

Now glory be unto our God
   all praise be justly given,
Ye humble souls that love the Lord
   Come seek the joys of Heaven.

Hartford, January 1, 1782.

AN
Evening's Improvement.

SHEWING,

The NECESSITY of beholding
the LAMB of GOD.

To which is added,

A DIALOGUE,

ENTITLED,

The KIND MASTER and
DUTIFUL SERVANT.

Written by JUPITER HAMMON, a Negro
Man belonging to Mr. *John Lloyd*, of Queen's
Village, on Long-Island, now in Hartford.

HARTFORD:
Printed for the Author, by the Assistance of his Friends.

A DIALOGUE ENTITLED THE KIND MASTER
AND THE DUTIFUL SERVANT

Master.

1. Come my servant, follow me,
   According to thy place;
   And surely God will be with thee,
   And send thee heav'nly grace.

Servant.

2. Dear Master, I will follow thee,
   According to thy word,
   And pray that God may be with me,
   And save thee in the Lord.

Master.

3. My Servant, lovely is the Lord,
   And blest those servants be,
   That truly love his holy word,
   And thus will follow me.

Servant.

4. Dear Master, that's my whole delight,
   Thy pleasure for to do;
   As for grace and truth's in sight,
   Thus far I'll surely go.

Master.

5.   My Servant, grace proceeds from God,
        And truth should be with thee;
      Whence e'er you find it in his word,
        Thus far come follow me.

Servant.

6.   Dear Master, now without controul,
        I quickly follow thee;
      And pray that God would bless thy soul,
        His heav'nly place to see.

Master.

7.   My Servant, Heaven is high above,
        Yea, higher than the sky:
      I pray that God would grant his love,
        Come follow me thereby.

Servant.

8.   Dear Master, now I'll follow thee,
        And trust upon the Lord;
      The only safety that I see,
        Is Jesus's holy word.

Master.

9.   My Servant, follow Jesus now,
        Our great victorious King;
      Who governs all both high and low,
        And searches things within.

Servant.

10.   Dear Master, I will follow thee,
      When praying to our King;
    It is the Lamb I plainly see,
      Invites the sinner in.

Master.

11.   My Servant, we are sinners all,
      But follow after grace;
    I pray that God would bless thy soul,
      And fill thy heart with grace.

Servant.

12.   Dear Master I shall follow then,
      The voice of my great King;
    As standing on some distant land,
      Inviting sinners in.

Master.

13.   My servant we must all appear,
      And follow then our King;
    For sure he'll stand where sinners are,
      To take true converts in.

Servant.

14.   Dear Master, now if Jesus calls,
      And sends his summons in;
    We'll follow saints and angels all,
      And come unto our King.

Master.

15.   My servant now come pray to God,
           Consider well his call;
       Strive to obey his holy word,
           That Christ may love us all.

       A Line *on the present* war.

Servant.

16.   Dear Master now it is a time,
           A time of great distress;
       We'll follow after things divine,
           And pray for happiness.

Master.

17.   Then will the happy day appear.
           That virtue shall increase;
       Lay up the sword and drop the spear,
           And Nations seek for peace.

Servant.

18.   Then shall we see the happy end,
           Tho' still in some distress;
       That distant foes shall act like friends,
           And leave their wickedness.

Master.

19.   We pray that God would give us grace,
           And make us humble too;
       Let ev'ry Nation seek for peace,
           And virtue make a show.

Servant.

20. Then we shall see the happy day,
        That virtue is in power;
     Each holy act shall have its sway,
        Extend from shore to shore.

Master.

21. This is the work of God's own hand,
        We see by precepts given;
     To relieve distress and save the land,
        Must be the pow'r of heav'n.

Servant.

22. Now glory be unto our God,
        Let ev'ry nation sing;
     Strive to obey his holy word,
        That Christ may take them in.

Master.

23. Where endless joys shall never cease,
        Blest Angels constant sing;
     The glory of their God increase,
        Hallelujahs to their King.

Servant.

24. Thus the Dialogue shall end,
        Strive to obey the word;
     When ev'ry Nation acts like friends,
        Shall be the sons of God.

25.   Believe me now my Christian friends,
          Believe your friend call'd Hammon:
       You cannot to your God attend,
          And serve the God of Mammon.

26.   If God is pleased by his own hand
          To relieve distresses here;
       And grant a peace throughout the the (*sic*) land,
          'Twill be a happy year.

27.   'Tis God alone can give us peace;
          It's not the pow'r of man:
       When virtuous pow'r shall increase,
          'Twill beautify the land.

28.   Then shall we rejoice and sing
          By pow'r of virtues word,
       Come sweet Jesus, heav'nly King,
          Thou art the Son of God.

29.   When virtue comes in bright array,
          Discovers ev'ry sin;
       We see the dangers of the day,
          And fly unto our King.

30.   Now glory be unto our God,
          All praise be justly given;
       Let ev'ry soul obey his word,
          And seek the joy of heav'n.

                         FINIS.

The Prose of Jupiter Hammon

A

WINTER PIECE:

BEING A

SERIOUS EXHORTATION,

WITH A CALL TO THE

UNCONVERTED:

AND A SHORT

CONTEMPLATION

ON THE

DEATH OF JESUS CHRIST.

WRITTEN BY

JUPITER HAMMON,

A NEGRO MAN belonging to Mr. JOHN LLOYD, of
Queen's Village, on Long Island, now in Hartford.

Published by the AUTHOR with the Assistance
of his Friends.

HARTFORD:
PRINTED FOR THE AUTHOR.
M.DCC.LXXXII.

A WINTER PIECE

As I have been desired to write something more than Poetry, I shall endeavour to write from these words, Matthew xi, 28. Come unto me all ye that labour and are heavy laden.

My Brethren, I shall endeavour by divine assistance, to shew what is meant by coming to the Lord Jesus Christ labouring and heavy laden, and to conclude, I shall contemplate on the death of Jesus Christ.

My Brethren, in the first place, I am to shew what is meant by coming to Christ labouring and heavy laden. We are to come with a sense of our own unworthiness, and to confess our sins before the most high God, and to come by prayer and meditation, and we are to confess Christ to be our Saviour and mighty Redeemer. Matthew x, 33. Whosoever shall confess me before men, him will I confess before my heavenly father. Here, my brethren, we have great encouragement to come to the Lord, and ask for the influence of his holy spirit, and that he would give us the water of eternal life, John iv. 14. Whosoever shall drink of this water as the woman of Samaria did, shall never thirst; but it shall be in them a well of water springing up to eternal life, then we shall believe in the merits of Christ, for our eternal salvation, and come labouring and heavy laden with a sense of our lost and undone state without an interest in the merits of Christ. It should be our greatest care to trust in the Lord, as David did, Psalm xxxi, 1. In thee O Lord put I my trust.

My Brethren, we must come to the divine fountain to
turn us from sin to holiness, and to give us grace to repent
of all our sins; this none can do but God. We must come
labouring and heavy laden not trusting to our own righteous-
ness, but we are to be cloathed with the righteousness of
Christ. Then may we apply this text, Psalm xxxiii, 7. Blessed
is he whose transgressions is forgiven, whose sins is covered.
This we must seek for by prayer and meditation, and we are
to pray without ceasing, and the word is set forth by David
in Psalm lxi, 1. Have mercy on me O God, according to
thy loving kindness, according unto the multitude of thy
tender mercies blot out my transgressions. My Brethren we
are to come poor in spirit.

In the second place in order to come to the divine foun-
tain labouring and heavy laden, we are to avoid all bad
company, to keep ourselves pure in heart.

Matthew v. 8. Blessed are the poor in heart for they
shall see God. Now, in order to see God we must have a
saving change wrought in our hearts, which is the work of
God's holy spirit which we are to ask for, Matthew vii, 7.
Ask and it shall be given you, seek and ye shall find. It
may be asked what shall we find? Ye will find the mercies
of God to allure you, the influence of his holy spirit to
guide you in the right way to eternal life, Matt. vii, 8. For
every one that asketh receiveth, but then my brethren we
are to ask in a right manner, with faith and repentance, for
except we repent we shall surely die, that is, we must suffer
the wrath of the most high God, who will turn you away
with this pronunciation depart from me ye workers of
iniquity, Matt. vii, 23. Therefore you see how dangerous a
thing it is to live in any known sin, either of commission
or omission, for if we commit any wilful sin, we become the
servants of sin John viii, 34. Whosoever committeth sin is
the servant of sin. My dear brethren, have we not rendered
ourselves too much the servants of sin, by a breach of

God's holy commandments, by breaking his holy Sabbath, when we should have been fitting for our great and last change? Have we not been amusing ourselves with the pleasures of this life, or, if we have attended divine service, have we been sincere? For God will not be mocked, for he knows our thoughts. John iv, 24, God is a spirit, and they that worship him must worship him in spirit and in truth. Therefore my Brethren, we see how necessary it is that we should be sincere when we attempt to come to the Lord whether in public service or private devotion, for it is not the outward appearance but sincerity of the heart. This we must manifest by a holy life; for it is not every one that says Lord, Lord, shall enter into the kingdom of Heaven; but he that doth the will of my heavenly Father, Matt. vii, 21.

Therefore, we ought to come labouring and heavy laden to the throne of grace, and pray that God may be pleased to transform us anew in Christ Jesus. But it may be objected by those who have had the advantage of studying, every one is not calculated for teaching of others. To those I answer, Sirs, I do not attempt to teach those who I know are able to teach me, but I shall endeavour by divine assistance to enlighten the minds of my brethren; for we are a poor despised nation, whom God in his wise providence has permitted to be brought from their native place to a christian land, and many thousands born in what are called christian families, and brought up to years of understanding. In answer to the objectors, Sirs, pray given me leave to enquire into the state of those children that are born in those christian families, have they been baptised, taught to read, and learnt their catechism? Surely this is a duty incumbent on masters or heads of families. Sirs, if you had a sick child, would you not send for a doctor? If your house was on fire would you not strive to put it out to save your interest? Surely then you ought to use the means appointed to save the souls

which God has committed to your charge, and not forget
the words of Joshua, as for me and my house we will serve
the Lord. Children should be taught the fear of God: See
what Solomon says, Prov. viii, 18. The fear of the Lord is
to hate evil; chapter ix, 10. The fear of the Lord is the
beginning of wisdom; chapter xiv, 17. The fear of the Lord
is a fountain of life. Here we see that children should fear
the Lord.

But I turn to my Brethren for whom this discourse is
designed. My Brethren, if ye are desirous to be saved by the
merits of Jesus Christ, ye must forsake all your sins, and
come to the Lord by prayer and repentance of all your
former sins, come labouring and heavy laden; for we are
invited to come and rely on the blessed Jesus for eternal
salvation. Matthew x, 32. Whosoever shall confess me before
men, him will I confess before my heavenly father. Here we
have our Saviour's words for our encouragement. See to it
my brethren, that ye live a holy life, and that ye walk more
circumspect or holy than ye have done heretofore. I now
assure you that God is a spirit, and they that worship him
must worship him in spirit and in truth; therefore if ye
would come unto him, come as the poor publican did, and
say God be merciful to me a sinner; Luke xv, 11. And the
publican standing afar off would not lift up so much as his
eyes unto heaven, but smote upon his breast saying, God
be merciful to me a sinner. For if we hope to be saved by
the merits of Jesus Christ, we cast off all self-dependence,
as to our own righteousness; for by grace ye are saved
through faith, and that not of yourselves, it is the gift of
God.

Here we see that the imperfections of human nature is
such, that we cannot be saved by any other way but the
name of Jesus Christ, and that there must be a principle of
love and fear of God implanted in our hearts, if we desire
to come to the divine fountain labouring and heavy laden

with our sins. But the enquirer may enquire how do you prove this doctrine, are you not imposing on your brethren, as you know many of them cannot read. To this I answer, Sir, I do not mean to impose on my brethren, but to shew them there must be a principle of fear and love to God, and now I am to prove this doctrine that we ought to fear God, Psalm ciii, 11. For as the heavens is high above the earth, so great is his mercy towards them that fear him. Verse 13. Like as a father pitieth his children, so the Lord pitieth them that fear him. Psalm xxxiv, 9. O fear the Lord ye his saints, for there is no want to them that fear him. Verse 11. Come ye children hearken unto me, I will teach you the fear of the Lord. This may suffice to prove the doctrine that we ought to fear the Lord, here by brethren we see how much our salvation depends on our being transformed anew in Christ Jesus, for we are sinners by nature and are adding thereunto every day of our life, for man is prone to evil as the sparks to fly upward, this thought should put us on our guard against all manner of evil, especially of bad company. This leads me to say, we should endeavour to glorify God in all our actions whether spiritual or temporal, for the apostle hath told us whatever we do, do all to the glory of God. 1 Cor. x, 30.

Let us now labour for that food which tendeth unto eternal life, this none can give but God only: My Brethren, it is your duty to strive to make your calling and election sure by a holy life, working out your salvation with fear and trembling, for we are invited to come without money and without price.

Isaiah lv, 1. Ho every one that thirsteth come ye to the waters; and he that hath no money, come ye buy and eat; yea come and buy wine and milk without money and without price. This leads me to say if we suffer as sinners, under the light of the gospel as sinners, the fault is in us, for our Saviour hath told us if he had not come we should not had

sin, but now they have no cloak for their sins. Let us now
improve our talents by coming labouring and burthened with
a sense of our sins. This certainly is a necessary duty of all
mankind, to come to the divine fountain for mercy and for
the influence of God's holy spirit to guide us through this
wilderness to the mansions of eternal glory.

My Brethren, have we not great encouragement to come
unto the Lord Jesus Christ, Matthew vii, 7. Ask and it shall
be given you, knock and it shall be opened unto you.
Therefore if ye desire to be saved by the merits of Christ,
ye must come as the prodigal son did, Luke xv, 21. And
the son said unto him father I have sinned against Heaven
and in thy sight, and am no more worthy to be called thy
son. This is the language of the true penetent, for he is
made sensible that there is no other name given by which he
can be saved, but by the name of Jesus. Therefore we
should put our trust in him and strive to make our calling
and election sure, by prayer and meditation. Psalm lv, 1.
Give ear to my prayer O God, and hide not thyself from
my supplication.

But, my Brethren, are we not too apt to put off the
thoughts of death till we are sick, or some misfortune
happens to us, forgetting that bountiful hand who gives us
every good gift: Doth not the tokens of mortality call aloud
to us all to prepare for death our great and last change, not
flattering ourselves with the hopes of a long life, for we
know not what a day may bring forth, therefore my Breth-
ren let it be your greatest care to prepare for death, that
great and irresistable king of terrors. Are we many of us
advanced in years and we know not how soon God may be
pleased to call us out of this life to an endless eternity, for
this is the lot of all men, once to die, and after that the
judgment. Let us now come to the Lord Jesus Christ, with
a sense of our own impotency to do any good thing of
ourselves, and with a thankful remembrance of the death of

Christ who died to save lost man, and hath invited us to
come to him labouring and heavy laden. My ancient Breth-
ren, let us examine ourselves now whither we have had a
saving change wrought in our hearts, and have repented of
our sins, have we made it our greatest care to honor God's
holy word and to keep his holy Sabbath's and to obey his
commandments.

Exodus xx, 6. And shewing mercy to thousands of them
that love me and keep my commandments, have we been
brought to bow to the divine sovereignty of the Most High
God and to fly to the arms of the crucified Jesus, at whose
crucification the mountains trembled, and the rocks rent, and
the graves were opened and many bodies of saints that slept
arose. Come my dear fellow servants and brothers, Africans
by nation, we are all invited to come, Acts x, 34. Then
Peter opened his mouth and said, of a truth I perceive that
God is no respecter of persons, verse 35, But in every nation
he that feareth him is accepted of him. My Brethren, many
of us are seeking a temporal freedom, and I wish you may
obtain it; remember that all power in heaven and on earth
belongs to God; if we are slaves it is by the permission of
God, if we are free it must be by the power of the most
high God. Stand still and see the salvation of God, cannot
that same power that divided the waters from the waters
for the children of Israel to pass through, make way for
your freedom, and I pray that God would grant your desire,
and that he may give you grace to seek that freedom which
tendeth to eternal life, John viii, 32, And ye shall know the
truth and the truth shall make you free. Verse 36, If the Son
shall make you free you shall be free indeed.

This we know my brethren, that all things work together
for good to them that love God. Let us manifest this love
to God by a holy life.

My dear Brethren, as it hath been reported that I had
petitioned to the court of Hartford against freedom, I now

solemnly declare that I never have said, nor done any thing, neither directly nor indirectly, to promote or to prevent freedom; but my answer hath always been I am a stranger here and I do not care to be concerned or to meddle with public affairs, and by this declaration I hope my friends will be satisfied, and all prejudice removed. Let us all strive to be united together in love, and to become new creatures, for if any man be in Christ Jesus he is a new creature, 2 Cor. v. 17. Therefore if any man be in Christ he is a new creature Old things are passed away behold all things are become new, now to be a new creature is to have our minds turned from darkness to light, from sin to holiness and to have a desire to serve God with our whole hearts, and to follow his precepts. Psalm xix, 10. More to be desired than gold, yea than much fine gold, sweeter than honey and the honey comb. Verse 11. Moreover by them is thy servant warned, and by keeping them there is great reward.

Let me now, my brethren, persuade you to prepare for death by prayer and meditation, that is the way Mat. vi. But when thou prayest enter into thy closet, and, when thou hast shut the door, pray to thy father in secret, and thy father which seeth in secret shall reward thee openly.

My Brethren, while we continue to sin we are enemies to Christ, ruining ourselves, and a hurt to the commonwealth.

Let us now, my brethren, come labouring and heavy laden with a sense of our sins, and let us pray that God may in his mercy be pleased to life up the gates of our hearts, and open the doors of our souls, that the King of Glory may come in, and set these things home on our hearts. Psalm xxiv. 7. Lift up your heads O ye gates, and be ye lifted us ye everlasting doors, and the King of Glory shall come in; then may we rely on the merits of Christ, and say, as David did, In the Lord put I my trust, Psalm xi. 4. And again, whom have I in heaven but thee, and there is none 'on earth I desire besides thee.

And now, my brethren, I shall endeavour to prove that we are not only ruining ourselves by sin, but many others. If the generality of men were more humble and more holy, we should not hear the little children in the street taking God's holy name in vain. Surely our conversation should be yea, yea, and nay, nay, or to that purpose. Matt. v. 7. But let your communication be yea, yea, nay, nay, for whatsoever is more than these cometh of evil. Therefore my Brethren, we should endeavor to walk humble and holy, to avoid the appearance of evil; to live a life void of offence toward God and towards man. Hear what David saith, Psalm i, 1. Blessed is the man that walketh not in the counsel of the ungodly nor standeth in the way of sinners. Here we see how much it becomes us to live as christians, not in rioting and drunkenness, uncleanness, Sabbath breaking, swearing, taking God's holy name in vain; but our delight should be in the law of the Lord.

The righteous man is compared to a tree that bringeth forth fruit in season. Psalm i, 3. And he shall be like a tree planted by the rivers of water, that bringeth forth fruit in his season: His leaf also shall not wither, and whatsoever he doeth shall prosper. Let us not forget the words of holy David, man is but dust like the flower of the field. Psalm ciii, 15.

Let us remember the uncertainty of human life, and that we are many of us within a step of the grave, hanging only by the single thread of life, and we know not how soon God may send the cold hand of death and cut the thread of life; Then will our souls either ascend up to the eternal mansions of glory or descend down to eternal misery, our bodies lodged in the cold and silent grave, numbered with the dead, then shall the scripture be fulfilled, Gen. iii. 19. In the sweat of thy face shalt thou eat bread, till thou return to the ground, for out of it wast thou taken, for dust thou art and unto dust thou shalt return.

Now I am to call to the unconverted, my brethren, if we desire to become true converts we must be born again, we must have a spiritual regeneration. John iii, 3. Verily, verily I say unto you, except a man be born again he cannot see the kingdom of God.

My brethren, are we not, many of us, ignorant of this spiritual regeneration? Have we seen our lost and undone condition without an interest in the merits of Jesus Christ; have we come weary and heavy laden with our sins, and to say with holy David, Psalm vi. 10. Lord rebuke me not in thine anger, neither chasten me in thy hot displeasure. Hath it been our great care to prepare for death our great and last change, by prayer and meditation.

My dear brethren, though we are servants and have not so much time as we could wish for, yet we must improve the little time we have.

Mr. Burket, a great divine of our church, says, a man's hand may be on his plow and his heart in heaven, by putting up such prayers and ejaculations as these, Psalm lxi. 1. Hear my cry O God, attend to my prayer, and again, Whom have I in heaven but thee, and there is none on earth I desire besides thee.

We should pray that God would give us his holy spirit, that we may not be lead into temptation, and that we may be delivered from evil, especially the evil of sin. Rom. vi. 22, 23. But now, being made free from sin, and become servants of God, ye have your fruit unto holiness, and the end everlasting life. For the wages of sin is death, but the gift of God is eternal life through Jesus Christ our Lord.

My brethren, seeing I am desired by my friends to write something more than poetry, give me leave to speak plainly to you. Except you repent and forsake your sins ye must surely die. Now we see how much it becomes us to break our alliance with sin and Satan, and to fly to a crucified Saviour, and to enlist under Christ's banner, and that he may give us grace to become his faithful subjects, should be our constant prayers. We should guard against every sin, especially against bad language.

Therefore, my Brethren, we should always be guarding against every evil word, for we are told that the tongue is an evil member, for with the tongue we bless God, and with the tongue we curse men. 1 Peter iii. 10. For he that loves life, and would see good days, let him refrain his tongue from evil and his lips from speaking guile. But the thoughtless and unconverted sinner is going on in open rebellion, against that divine power which can in one minute cut the thread of life, and cast them away with this pronunciation, Depart from me ye workers of iniquity. Matt. xxv. 41. Then shall he say also unto them on the left hand, depart from me ye cursed into everlasting fire prepared for the devil and his angels.

And now, by brethren, shall we abuse the divine sovereignty of a holy God, who hath created us rational creatures, capable of serving him under the light of the Gospel, for he hath told us if he had not come unto us we had not had sin, but now we have no cloak for our sin.

Come now my dear brethren, accept of Jesus Christ on the terms of the gospel, which is by faith and repentance. Come labouring and heavy laden with your sins, and a sense of your unworthiness.

My Brethren, it is not we servants only that are unworthy, but all mankind by the fall of Adam, became guilty in the sight of God. Gen. ii. 17. Surely then we are sinners by nature, and are daily adding thereto by evil practices, and it is only by the merits of Jesus Christ we can be saved, we are told that he is a Jew that is a Jew in his heart, so he is a Christian that is a Christian in his heart, and it is not every one that says Lord, Lord, shall enter into the kingdom of God, but he that doth the will of God. Let our superiors act as they shall think it best, we must resolve to walk in

the steps our Saviour hath set before us, which was a holy
life, a humble submission to the will of God. Luke xxii.
41, 42. And he was withdrawn from them about a stones
cast, and he kneeled down and prayed saying, father if thou
be willing remove this cup from me, nevertheless not my
will but thine be done.

Here we have the example of our Saviour who came down
from heaven to save mankind, lost and undone without an
interest in the merits of Jesus Christ, the blessed Jesus then
gave his life a ransom for all that come unto him by faith
and repentance; and shall not he that spared not his own
son, but delivered him up for us all, with him freely give
all things.

Come let us seek first, Christ, the kingdom of God; and
his righteousness, all other things shall be added unto you.
Matt. vi. 33. Here we have great encouragement to come to
the divine fountain.

Bishop Beverage says, in his third resolution, the eyes of
the Lord is intent upon us, he seeth our actions; if our sins
are not washed out with our tears, and crost with the blood
of Christ, we cannot be saved. Come my brethren, O taste
and see that the Lord is good, and blessed is the man that
trusteth in him. Psalm xxxiv. 8. Let us not stand as Felix
did, and say, almost thou persuadest me to be a christian,
but, let us strive to be altogether so. If ye desire to become
converts you must have a saving change wrought in your
hearts that shall bring forth good works meet for repentance:
Acts iii. 19. Repent ye therefore, be converted: We are not
to trust in our own strength but to trust in the Lord;
Proverbs iii, 4. "Trust in the Lord with all thine heart, and
lean not unto thine own understanding."

My brethren, are we not incircled with many temptations,
the flesh, the world and the devil; these must be resisted at
all times. We must see to it that we do not grieve the holy
spirit of God. Come let us my dear brethren, draw near to

the Lord by faith and repentance, for faith without works is dead. James ii. 20. and Rom. x, 10. For with the heart man believeth, and with the mouth confession is made unto salvation. Here we see there is something to be done by us as Christians; therefore we should walk worthy of our profession, not forgetting that there is a divine power which takes a just survey of all our actions, and will reward every one according to their works. Psalm lxii, 2. "Also unto the Lord belongeth mercy, for thou rememberest every man according to his works." Therefore, it is our indispensable duty to improve all opportunities to serve God, who gave us his only son to save all that come unto him by faith and repentance.

Let me, my brethren, persuade you to a serious consideration of your danger while you continue in an unconverted state. Did you feel the operations of God's holy spirit, you then would leave all for an interest in the merits of Christ; "For the kingdom of heaven is like a treasure hid in a field; for which a man will sell all that he hath to purchase, Matt. x. 44. So will every true penitent part with all for the sake of Christ. I shall not attempt to drive you to Christ by the terrors of the law, but I shall endeavour to allure you by the invitation of the gospel, to come labouring and heavy laden.

Matt. xi. 27. Man at his best estate is like a shadow of the field. We should always be preparing for death, not having our hearts set on the things of this life: For what profit will it be to us, to gain the whole world and loose his own soul. Matt. xvi. 26. We should be always preparing for the will of God, working out our salvation with fear and trembling. O may we abound in the works of the Lord. Let us not stand as fruitless trees or cumberers of the ground, for by your works you shall be justified, and by your works you shall be condemned; for every man shall be rewarded according to his works, Matt. xvi. 27. Let us then be press-

ing forward to the mark, for the prize of the high calling of
God in Christ Jesus. Let our hearts be fixed where true joys
are to be found. Let us lay up treasures in Heaven, where
neither moth nor rust doth corrupt, nor thieves break
through nor steal. Matt. vi. 20.

Now I am come to contemplate the death of Christ, it
remains I make a short contemplation. The death of Christ
who died! Died to save lost man, 1 Cor. xv. 21. "For since
by man came death, by man came also the resurrection from
the dead: For as in Adam all died even so in Christ, shall
all be made alive." Let us turn to the scriptures, and there
we shall see how our Saviour was denied by one and be-
trayed by another. Matt. xxvi, 14. Judas went unto the
Chief Priest, and said, what will you give me, and they
agreed for thirty pieces of silver, then they sought oppor-
tunity to betray him. Verse 28. For this is my blood of the
New Testament, which is shed for many for the remission
of sins. Ver. 33. Peter answered and said unto him, though
all men should be offended because of thee, yet will I never
be offended. Ver. 34. Jesus said unto him, verily I say unto
thee, this night before the cock crow, thou shalt deny me
thrice. Ver. 38, Then saith he unto them, my soul is ex-
ceeding sorrowful, even unto death: tarry ye here and watch
with me. Ver. 39. And he went a little further and fell on
his face and prayed, saying, O Father, if it be possible, let
this cup pass from me: Nevertheless not as I will, but as
thou wilt.

My Brethren, here we see the love of God plainly set
before us; that while we were yet sinners, he sent his son
to die for all those that come unto him, labouring and heavy
laden with a sense of their sins; let us come with a thankful
remembrance of his death, whose blood was shed for us
guilty worms of the dust. Matt. xxvi. 63. But Jesus held his
peace, and the High Priest answered and said unto him, I
adjure thee by the Living God, that thou tell us, whether

thou be the Christ the son of God. And ver. 64. Jesus saith
unto him, thou hast said: nevertheless I say unto you,
hereafter shall ye see the Son of Man sitting on the right
hand of power, and coming in the clouds of heaven. Ver.
64. Then the High Priest rent his clothes, saying, he hath
spoken blasphemy; what further need have we of witness:
Behold, now ye have heard his blasphemy. Here the High
Priest charged the blessed Jesus with blasphemy: But we
must believe that he is able to save all that come unto him,
by faith and repentance. Matt. xxviii. 18. And Jesus came
and spoke unto them, saying, all power is given unto me in
heaven and on earth. As this should excite us to love and
fear God, and to strive to keep his holy commandments,
which is the only rule of life: But how apt are we to forget
that God spoke these words, saying, I am the Lord thy
God, which brought thee out of the land of Egypt and out
of the house of bondage, Exod. xx. 1. Thus we see how
the children of Israel were delivered from the Egyptian
service.

But my Brethren, we are invited to the blessed Jesus, who
was betrayed by one and denied by another. Matt. xx. 24.
The Son of Man goeth as it is written of him; but woe unto
that man by whom the Son of Man is betrayed; it had been
good for that man if he had never been born. Ver. 24. Then
Judas which betrayed him answered and said, Master is it I?
He said unto him, thou hast said.

Thus we see, my Brethren, that there is a woe pronounced
against every one that sins by omission or commission, are
we not going on in our sins, and disobeying the word of
God: "If ye love me, ye will keep my commandments."
Are we not denying the Lord Jesus, as Peter did. Matt.
xxvi. 14. Then began he to curse and swear, saying, I know
not the man; and immediately the cock crew. And ver. 74.
And Peter remembered the words of Jesus, which he said
unto him, before the cock crow thou shalt deny me thrice:

And he went out and wept bitterly. Surely then we ought
to come to the Divine Sovereign, the blessed Jesus who was
crucified for us sinners. Oh! we ought to come on the
bended knees of our souls, and say, Lord, we believe, help
thou our unbelief. Come my Brethren, let us cry to the life
giving Jesus, and say, Son of God, have mercy on us! Lamb
of God, that taketh away the sins of the world, have mercy
on us! Let us cast off all self-dependence, and rely on a
crucified Saviour. Luke xxiii. 20. Pilate therefore, willing to
release Jesus, spoke again to them. Ver. 21. But they cried,
saying, crucify him, crucify him. Here we may see the love
of God, in giving his Son to save all that come unto him by
faith and repentance. Let us trace the sufferings of our
Saviour a little further: Matt. xxvi. 42. He went away
again the second time, and prayed, saying, O my Father,
if this cup may not pass away from me, except I drink it,
thy will be done. Here we trace our Saviour's example set
before us; so that we should not murmur at the hand of
Divine Providence; for God hath a right to deal with his
creatures as he pleaseth.

Come let us contemplate on the death of the blessed
Jesus; and on the fearful judgment of the Lord passing on
the guilty sinner. Luke xxiii. 30. Then shall they begin to
say to the mountains, fall on us, and to the hills, cover us.
Ver. 32, 33. And there were also two malefactors led with
him to be put to death; and when they were come to the
place, which is called Calvary, there they crucified him and
the malefactors, one on the right hand, and the other on the
left; and thus was the scripture fulfilled: For he was num-
bered with transgressors. Matt. xxvii. 29. And when they
had plated a crown of thorns, they put it upon his head,
and a reed in his right hand. Ver. 41, 42. Likewise the Chief
Priests mocking him, with the Scribes and Elders, said, he
saved others, himself he cannot save: If he be the king of
Israel, let him come down from the cross, and we will

believe him. Ver. 44. Now from the sixth hour there was
darkness over all the land unto the ninth hour. Ver. 46.
And about the ninth hour Jesus cried with a loud voice,
saying, Eli, Eli, Lama Sabachthani! That is to say, my God,
my God, why hast thou forsaken me?

My brethren, should not a sense of these things on our mind
implant in us a spirit of love to God, which hath provided
a Saviour, who is able to save to the uttermost all that come
unto him by faith and repentance. 2. Cor. vii. 10. For
Godly sorrow worketh repentance to salvation, not to be
repented of, but the sorrow of the world worketh death. My
brethren, see what sin hath done; it hath made all flesh
guilty in the sight of God.

May we not adopt the language of David. Psal. lxxix 8.
O remember not against us former iniquities. Let they tender
mercies speedily prevent us. Psal. lxxx 19. Turn us again,
O Lord, God of Hosts, cause thy face to shine, and we shall
be saved.

Let us contemplate a little further on the death of Christ.
Matt. xxvii. 40. Jesus, when he had cried with a loud voice,
yielded up the ghost. Ver. 4, And behold the vail of the
temple was rent in twain, from the top to the bottom; and
the earth did quake, and the rocks rent. Here we see that
the death of Christ caused all nature to tremble, and the
power of heaven shaken: Here we may see not only the evil
of sin, but also the unmeritted mercy of God, in giving his
only Son. Should not our hearts be filled with fear and love
to God; and we must believe that Jesus is the Son of God.
Matt. xxvii. 54. Now when the Centurion and they that
were with him, watching Jesus saw the earth quake, and
those things that were done, they feared greatly, saying, truly
this was the Son of God. Now this was done for the re-
mission of our sins, for without shedding of blood there is
no remission of sin. This we have confirmed in the holy
sacrament. Matt. xxvi. 27. For this is my blood of the New

Testament, which was shed for many: But the unbelieving
Jews still persisted in their unbelief, and would have prevented
the resurrection of our Saviour, if it had been in their
power. Matt. xxvii. 62. The Chief Priests and Pharisees
come together unto Pilate. Ver. 63, Saying, Sir, we remem-
ber that that deceiver said, while he was yet alive, after three
days I will rise again. Ver. 66. So they went and made the
sepulchre sure, sealing the stone and setting a watch. Here
we see the spirit of unbelief in Nathaniel. John i. 45 and 46.
Philip findeth Nathaniel, and saith unto him, we have found
him, of whom Moses in the law of the prophets did write,
Jesus of Nazareth, the son of Joseph: And Nathaniel said
unto him, can there any good thing come out of Nazareth?
Philip saith unto him, come and see. Thus we are to come
and see the mercy of God, in sending his Son to save lost
men. Let us contemplate on the manner of Christ's resur-
rection. Matt. xxv. 2. Behold there was a great earthquake;
for the angel of the Lord descended from heaven, and come
and rolled the stone from the door, and sat upon it. Here
we see that our Saviour was attended by an angel; one of
those holy spirits we read of in the Revelations, vi. 8. They
rest not day and night, saying, holy, holy, holy Lord God
Almighty, which was and is, and is to come. Ver. 4, 12.
Saying, with a loud voice, worthy is the Lamb, that was
slain, to receive power and riches, and wisdom, and strength,
and honor, and glory, and blessing. And our Saviour himself
tells us he hath received his power. Matt. xxviii 19. And
Jesus came and spoke unto them, saying, all power is given
unto me in heaven and in earth. Then he gives his disci-
ples their charge. Ver. 19. Go ye, therefore, and teach all
nations, baptizing then in the name of the Father, of the
Son, and of the Holy Ghost. But I must conclude in a few
words, and say,

My dear Brethren, should we not admire the free grace
of God, that he is inviting of us to come and accept of

Jesus Christ, on the terms of the gospel; and he is calling us to repent of all our sins: This we cannot do of ourselves, but we must be saved in the use of means not to neglect those two great articles of the Christian religion, baptism and the sacrament; and we ought all of us to seek by prayers: But the scripture hath told us, that we must not depend on the use of means alone. 1st Cor. iii. 6. The apostle says, I have planted Apolos watered, but God gave the increase. Here we see if we are saved, it must be by the power of God's holy spirit. But my dear Brethren the time is hastening when we must appear.

AN EVENING'S IMPROVEMENT

JOHN I. 29.

*— Behold the Lamb of God which taketh
away the sins of the world.*

In the begining of this chapter John bears testimony, that
Jesus is the Son of God. Verse 1st. In the begining was the
word, and the word was with God, and the word was God.
This is that Lamb of God which I now invite you to behold.
My Brethren, we are to behold the Son of God as our Lord
and giver of life; for he was made flesh and dwelt among
us, verse 14 of the context, and here he is declared to be
the Son of God full of grace and truth. And here in the
first place I mean to shew the necessity of beholding the
Lamb of God in the sense of the text. 2d. Endeavour to
shew when we are said to behold the Son of God in the
sense of the text. 3. I shall shew when we may be said not
to behold the Lamb of God as we should do. In the 4th
place I shall endeavor to shew how far we may be mistaken
in beholding the Lamb of God. In the 5th place I shall
endeavor to rectify these mistakes.

My brethren, since I wrote my Winter Piece it hath been
requested that I would write something more for the advan-
tage of my friends, by my superiors, gentlemen, whose
judgment I depend on, and by my friends in general, I have
had an invitation to give a public exhortation; but did not

think it my duty at that time; but now, by brethren, by divine assistance, I shall endeavor to shew the necessity of beholding the Lamb of God. My brethren we must behold the Lamb of God as taking away the sin of the world, as in our text, and it is necessary that we behold the Lamb of God as our King: ah! as the King immortal, eternal, invisible, as the only Son of God, for he hath declared him, as in the 8th verse of the context, no man hath seen God at any time: The only begotten Son, which is in the bosom of the Father, he hath declared him. My brethren, let us strive to behold the Lamb of God, with faith and repentance; to come weary and heavy laden with our sin, for they have made us unworthy of the mercy of the Lamb of God; therefore, we see how necessary it is that we behold the Lamb of God, in the sense of the text, that is, in a spiritual manner, not having on our own righteousness; but we must be cloathed upon, with the unspotted robes of the Lamb of God; we must work out our salvation with fear and trembling, always abounding in the works of the Lord; we must remember the vows of our baptism, which is to follow the Lamb of God. John Chap. 1. 33, speaking of baptism, he saith, upon whom thou shalt see the spirit descending and remaining on him, the same is he which baptiseth with the Holy Ghost, and verse 34, and I saw, and bare record, that this is the Son of God, verse 35, again the next day after, John stood and two of his disciples, verse 36, and looking upon Jesus, as he walked, and saith, behold the Lamb of God, verse 37, and the two disciples heard him speak and they followed Jesus. Thus, my dear brethren, we are to follow the Lamb of God, at all times, whether in prosperity of adversity, knowing that all things work together for good, to them that love God, or as in Rom. viii. 28. now let us manifest that we love God, by a holy life; let us strive to glorify and magnify the name of the most high God. It is necessary that we behold the Lamb of God, by taking heed

to our ways, that we sin not with our tongues, Psalm xxxix.
1. Here, by brethren, we have the exhortation of David, who
beheld the Lamb of God with faith and love, for he crys
out with a most humble petition, O Lord, rebuke me not in
thine anger; neither chastise me in thy hot displeasure.
Psalm vi. 1. and now, my brethren, have we not great rea-
son to cry to the Lamb of God, that taketh away the sin
of the world, that he may have mercy on us and forgive us
our sins, and that he would give us his holy spirit, that we
may have such hungerings and thirsting as may be acceptable
in the sight of God; for as the heart panteth for the water
brook, so should our souls pant for the living God. Psalm
xlii. 1. and now, my brethren, we must behold the law of
God, as is exprest, John I. 51. And he saith unto him,
verily, verily I say unto you, hereafter you shall see heaven
open, and the angels of God ascending and descending upon
the Son of Man. This is a representation of the great day,
when the Lamb of God shall appear. Matt. xxiv. 30, and
then shall appear the sign of the Son of Man in heaven, and
then shall the tribes of the earth mourn, and they shall see
the Son of Man coming in the clouds of heaven, with power
and great glory. Here my brethren, we have life and death
set before us, for if we mourn with the tribes for our sins,
which have made us unworthy of the least favour in the
sight of God, then he will have mercy and he will give us
his holy spirit; then we shall have hearts to pray to the
Lamb of God, as David did when he was made sensible of
his imperfections, then he cryed to the Lamb of God, have
mercy upon me O God, Psal. lxi. 1, according to thy loving
kindness, according to the multitude of thy tender mercies,
blot out my transgressions. This my brethren is the language
of the penitent, for he hath a desire that his heart may be
turned from darkness to light, from sin to holiness; this none
can do but God; for the carnal mind is enmity against God,
for it is not subject to the law of God, neither can be. Here

we see that we must behold the Lamb of God as calling to
us in the most tender and compassionate manner, Matt.
xxiii. 37, saying, O Jerusalem, Jerusalem, how often would
I have gathered thy children together, even as a hen gather-
eth her chickens under her wings, and ye would not. As
much as if he had said, O ye wicked and rebellious people
have I not sent the ministers of the gospel to teach you, and
you will not receive the doctrine of the gospel, which is
faith and repentance, I tell you nay; but except ye repent
ye shall all likewise perish, Luke xiii. 4.

And now my dear brethren, have we repented of our
sins? Have we not neglected to attend divine service? Or if
we have attended to the word of God, have we been sin-
cere? For God is a spirit, and they that worship him must
worship him in spirit and truth, John iv. 24. When we have
heard the word of God sounding in our ears, inviting of us
to behold the Lamb of God; O my dear brethren, have we
as it were laid up these words in our hearts, or have we
not been like the stony ground hearers? Matt. xii. 20. But
he that received the seed into stony places, the same is he
that heareth the word, and anon with joy receiveth it.
Ver. 21. Yet hath not root in himself, but dureth for a
while; for when tribulation or persecution ariseth because of
the word, by and by he is offended. This is the effect of a
hard heart. There is such a depravity in our natures that we
are not willing to suffer any reproach that may be cast on
us for the sake of our religion; this my brethren is because
we have not the love of God shed abroad in our hearts;
but our hearts are set too much on the pleasures of this
life, forgetting that they are passing away; but the children
of God are led by the spirit of God. Rom. viii. 12, There-
fore brethren we are debtors, not to the flesh to live after
the flesh. Ver. 13. For if ye live after the flesh ye shall
die; but if through the spirit do mortify the deeds of the
body, ye shall live. Ver. 14, For as many are led by the

spirit of God, they are the sons of God. Here my brethren we see that it is our indispensible duty to conform to the will of God in all things, not having our hearts set on the pleasures of this life; but we must prepare for death, our great and last change. For we are sinners by nature, and are adding thereunto by evil practices; for man is prone to evil as the sparks fly upward; and there is nothing short of the divine power of the most high God can turn our hearts to see the living and true God; and now we ought to behold the Lamb of God, as it is expressed in Isaiah vii. 14, A virgin shall conceive and bear a son, and shall call his name Emanuel. This my brethren is the Son of God, who died to save us guilty sinners, and it is only by the mercy of the blessed Jesus we can be saved: Therefore, let us cast off self-dependence, and rely on a crucified Saviour, whose blood was shed for all that came unto him by faith and repentance; this we cannot do of ourselves, but we must be found in the use of means; therefore we ought to come as David did, Psal. li. 1, Have mercy on me O God, according to thy loving kindness. This my brethren is the duty of all flesh to come to the divine fountain, and to confess our sins before the most high God; for if we say we have no sin we deceive ourselves and the truth is not in us; but if we confess our sins he is faithful and just to forgive us our transgressions. And now my brethren, seeing I have had an invitation to write something more to encourage my dear fellow servants and brethren, Africans, in the knowledge of the Christian religion, I must beg your patience, for I mean to use the utmost brevity that so important a subject will admit of; and now my brethren, we have, as I observed in the foregoing part of this discourse, life and death set before us, for we are invited to come and accept of Christ on the terms of the gospel. Isaiah xliv. 1, O every one that thirsteth, come ye to the waters, and he that hath no money, come ye buy and eat, yea, come ye buy wine and milk,

without money and without price. Here is life, and if we
search our hearts, and try our ways, and turn again unto
the Lord he will forgive us our sins and blot out our trans-
gressions, Lamen. iii. 40. But if we continue in our sins,
having our hearts set on the pleasures of this life, forgetting
that we must give an account for the deeds done in the
body. Psal. lxii. 12, Also unto the Lord belongeth mercy,
for he rendereth to every man according to his works. Here
we see that we should behold the Lamb of God by a holy
life. Psal. vii. 11, God judgeth the righteous and is angry
with the wicked every day, ver. 12, if he turn not. He will
whet his sword, he hath bent his bow and made it ready.
Here we see that the wrath of God abideth on the unbe-
lievers and unconverted sinner. And now my brethren,
should not a sense of these things make us cry out in the
apostle's language, 'Men and brethren what shall we do to
be saved?' We must be found in the use of means, and pray
that God would be pleased to rain down a rain of righteous-
ness into our souls; then we shall behold the Lamb of God
as taking away the sins of the world. Let us my brethren
examine ourselves whether we have had a saving change
wrought in our hearts, and have been brought to bow to the
divine sovereignty of a crucified Saviour; have we been
brought to behold the Lamb of God, by obeying the pre-
cepts of Isaiah, and turning from evil and learning to do
well. Isaiah i. 16, Wash ye, make you clean; put away the
evil of your doing from before mine eyes; cease to do evil,
learn to do well. Here we have the admonition of the proph-
et Isaiah, who was inspired with the knowledge of divine
things, so that he calls heaven and earth to witness against the
wicked and rebellious sinner. Isaiah i. 2, Here O heavens and
give ear O earth; for the Lord hath spoken, I have nourished
up children, and they have rebelled against me. Is not this the
case? Have we not been going astray like lost sheep? Luke
xv. 6, Have we not great reason to lay our hands on our

mouths and our mouths in the dust, and come upon the
bended knees of our souls and beg for mercy as the publican
did, saying, God be merciful to me a sinner, Luke viii. 13.
This my dear brethren should be the language of our con-
versation; to have a life void of offence towards God and
towards man. Have we beheld the Lamb of God, by taking
up our cross, denying ourselves, and following the blessed
Jesus. Matt. xvi. 24, Then said Jesus unto his disciples, if
any man will be my disciple, let him deny himself, take up
his cross and follow me. Here we see that we should behold
the Lamb of God as our only Saviour and mighty Re-
deemer, and we are to take up our cross and follow the
Lamb of God at all times, not to murmur at the hand of
Divine Providence; and we have our example set before us,
Luke xxii. 41, 42, And he was withdrawn from them about
a stone's cast, and he kneeled down and prayed, saying,
my Father, if thou be willing, remove this cup from me,
nevertheless not my will but thine be done. We should
behold the Lamb of God as coming in the clouds of heaven
with great power and glory, whom our heavenly Father hath
declared to be his only Son. Matt. xvii. 5, And while he
yet spoke, behold a bright cloud overshadowed them; and
behold a voice out of the cloud which said, this is my
beloved Son in whom I am well pleased, hear him. Should
not a sense of these things inflame our hearts with fear and
love to God; knowing that there is no other name given
by which we can be saved, but by the name of Jesus; let
us behold the Lamb of God as having power to make the
blind to see, the dumb to speak, and the lame to walk, and
even to raise the dead: But it may be objected and said by
those that have had the advantage of studying, are we to
expect miracles at this day? These things were done to con-
firm that Jesus was the Son of God, and to free us from
the burthen of types and ceremonies of the Jewish law; and
this by way of instruction, which I desire to receive with

an humble spirit. Others may object and say, what can we
expect from an unlearned Ethiopian? And this by way of
reflection. To this I answer, Pray Sir, give me leave to ask
this question, Doth not the raising of Lazarus give us a
sight of our sinful natures? John xi. 12, 13, And when he
had thus spoken, he said with a loud voice, Lazarus
come forth. Ver. 4, And he that was dead came forth,
bound hand and foot with grave clothes, and his head
was bound with a napkin; Jesus saith unto them, loose
him and let him go. Is not this a simile of our deadness by
nature? And there is nothing short of the power of the most
high God can raise us to life. Sirs, I know we are not to
expect miracles at this day; but hear the words of our
Saviour Matt. xvi. 16, And Simon Peter answered and said,
thou art Christ the Son of the living God. Ver. 17, And
Jesus answered and said unto him, blessed art thou Simon
Barjona, for flesh and blood hath not revealed it unto thee,
but my Father which is in heaven. Sirs, this may suffice to
prove that it is by grace we are saved, and that not of
ourselves, is the gift of God. But my brethren, for whom
this discourse is designed, I am now in the second place to
shew when we are said to behold the Lamb of God in the
sense of the text: When we are brought humbly to confess
our sins, before the most high God, and are calling on our
souls and all that is within us to bless his holy name; this
is the duty of all flesh, to praise God for his unmerited
mercy in giving his Son to save lost man, who by the fall
of Adam became guilty in the sight of God. Rom. v. 8,
But God commandeth his love towards us, in that while we
were sinners Christ died for us. Here we are to behold the
Lamb of God as suffering for our sins, and it is only by
the precious blood of Christ we can be saved, when we are
made sensible of our own imperfections and are desirous to
love and fear God; this we cannot do of ourselves, for this
is the work of God's holy spirit. John vi. 64, And he said,

therefore said I unto you that no man can come unto me
except it were given unto him of my Father. Here we see to
behold the Lamb of God, in the sense of the text, as the
gift of God; we should come as David did, saying, O Lord
rebuke me not in thine anger, neither chastise me in thy hot
displeasure, Psal. vi. 1. And we should put our whole trust
in the Lord at all times; we should strive to live a religious
life, to avoid the very appearance of evil, least we incur the
wrath of God. Psal. xi. 6, Upon the wicked he shall rain
showers of fire and brimstone, and an horrible tempest; this
shall be the portion of their cup. Here we see the unhappy
state of the sinner; for he is not only led away by that sub-
tle adversary the devil, but he hath the word of God pro-
nounced against him. Matt. xxv. 40, Then shall he say unto
them on the left hand depart from me ye cursed into ever-
lasting fire prepared for the devil and his angels. Here my
brethren we are to behold the Lamb of God as being cruci-
fied for us. Matt. xxiii. 20, Pilate therefore willing to release
Jesus spake again to them. ver. 22, But they cryed, saying
crucify him, crucify him. Here we see the effect of sin; the
blood of Christ was shed for all that came unto him by
faith and repentance. O my brethren, when those things
have a proper influence on our minds, by the power of the
most high God, to say as David did, Psal. ciii. 1, Bless the
Lord O my soul, and forget not all his benefits. Then we
may be said to behold the Lamb of God in the sense of the
text: And we are to behold the Lamb of God as it is
expressed in Matt. xvii. 22, And while they abode in Galil-
lee Jesus said unto them, the Son of Man shall be betrayed
into the hands of men; and ver. 23, And they shall kill
him, and the third day he shall rise again. And now should
not a sense of these things have a tendency to make us
humble in the sight of God, and we should see the place
and situation of Christ suffering. Luke xxii. 33, And when
they were come to the place called Calvary, there they

crucified him, and the malefactors one on the right hand
and the other on the left. Here we see the boundless riches
of free grace; he is numbered with transgressors, whose
blood speaks better things than the blood of Abel; for the
blood of Abel calls for justice on the sinner, but the blood
of Christ calls for mercy. Luke xxiii. 34, Then said Jesus,
Father forgive them, for they know not what they do. Here
we have the example of our Saviour, that we should forgive
our enemies, and pray that God would forgive them also, or
how shall we say the Lord's Prayer, 'Forgive us our tres-
passes as we forgive them that trespass against us.' Now
when we are enabled to do these things, as we should do
them, then may we be said to behold the Lamb of God in
the sense of the text. And now my dear brethren, I am to
remind you of a most melancholy scene of Providence; it
hath pleased the most high God, in his wise providence, to
permit a cruel and unnatural war to be commenced; let us
examine ourselves whether we have not been the cause of
this heavy judgment; have we been truly thankful for mercies
bestowed? And have we been humbled by afflictions? For
neither mercies nor afflictions proceed from the dust, but
they are the works of our heavenly Father; for it may be
that when the tender mercies of God will not allure us,
afflictions may drive us to the divine fountain. Let us now
cast an eye back for a few years and consider how many
hundreds of our nation and how many thousands of other
nations have been sent out of time into a never-ending
eternity, by the force of the cannon and by the point of the
sword. Have we not great cause to think this is the just
deserving of our sins; for this is the word of God. Isaiah
iii. 11, Woe unto the wicked, it shall be ill with him, for
the reward of his hands shall be given him. Here we see
that we ought to pray, that God may hasten the time when
the people shall beat their swords into plough-shares and
their spears into pruning-hooks, and nations shall learn war
no more.

And now my dear brethren have we not great reason to be thankful that God in the time of his judgments hath remembered mercy, so that we have the preaching of the Gospel and the use of our bibles, which is the greatest of all mercies; and if after all these advantages we continue in our sins, have we not the greatest reason to fear the judgments of God will be fulfilled on us. He that being often reproved hardneth his neck shall suddenly be destroyed, and that without remedy. Have we not great reason to praise God that he is giving us food and raiment, and to say as David did, Psal. cxxxvii. 1, O give thanks unto the Lord, for his mercy endureth for ever. And now my brethren, when these things make us more humble and more holy, then we may be said to behold the Lamb of God in the sense of the text. And now, in the third place, I am to shew when we may be said not to behold the Lamb of God in the sense of the text: When we are negligent to attend the word of God, and unnecessarily, or are living in any known sin, either of omission or commission, or when we have heard the word preached to us and have not improved that talent put into our hands by a holy life, then we may be said not to behold the Lamb of God in the sense of the text. And now my brethren, I am in the fourth place, to shew how in some things we may be mistaken in beholding the Lamb of God, while we are flattering ourselves with the hopes of salvation on the most slight foundation, because we live in a Christian land and attend to divine service; these things are good in themselves; but there must be a saving change wrought in our hearts, and we must become as new in Christ Jesus; we must not live after the flesh, but after the spirit, for as many as are led by the spirit of God are the sons of God, Rom. viii. 14. and we are to pray that God would keep us from all evil, especially the evil of sin. Bishop Bevrage, in his second Resolution, speaking of sin, he says, "For as God is the centre of all good, so sin is the fountain of all

evil in the world, all strife and contention, ignominy and
disgrace." Read a little further, and he goes on to protest
against sin, "I resolve to hate sin (says he) wherever I find
it, whether in myself or in others, in the best of my friends
as well as in the worst of my enemies." Here we see my
brethren that if we commit any willful sin, either of omis-
sion or commission, we become the servants of sin, and are
deceiving ourselves, for the apostle hath told us, that the
wages of sin is death, Rom. vi. 22, 23; but now being made
free from sin, and are become the servants of God ye have
your fruits into holiness, and in the end eternal life; for the
wages of sin is death, but the gift of God is eternal life
through Jesus Christ our Lord. We are to behold the Lamb
of God by reading the scriptures, and we must believe that
he hath power to give everlasting life. John vi. 47, Verily,
verily I say unto you, he that believeth on me hath ever-
lasting life. Do we my brethren believe in the blessed Jesus
as we ought? Are we not going the broad way to utter
destruction? Are we not leaving the blessed Jesus, who hath
the bread of life and is that bread? John vi. 48, I am the
bread of life. Here we see that the blessed Jesus hath power
to give eternal life to all that come unto him by faith and
repentance; and we see that he is calling to us as he did to
his disciples, saying, Wilt thou go away also; for this is the
language of the scriptures, John vi. 67, 68, Then Simon
answered him, Lord to whom shall we go? Thou hast the
words of eternal life. And we are my brethren to behold the
Lamb of God as being the door of eternal life, for this he
hath declared in his word to us. John x. 9, I am the door,
by me if any man enter he shall be saved, and shall go in
and out and find pasture. But it is very plain my brethren
that if we come in our sins God will not hear us, but if we
come and worship him in spirit and in truth he will have
mercy on us. John ix. 31, 32, Now we know that God
heareth not sinners, but if any man be a worshipper of God

and doth his will, him he heareth. My dear brethren as I am drawing to a conclusion, let me press on you to prepare for death, that great and irresistable king of terrors, by a holy life, and make the word of God the rule of your life; but it may be objected we do not understand the word of God. Mr. Burkit, a great divine of our church says, in the scriptures there is depths that an elephant may swim, and shoals that a lamb may wade. Therefore we must take the plainest text as a key to us. And now my brethren I am in the fifth place to endeavour to rectify any mistake we may labour under, when we are taking on us the form of Godliness, without the power thereof, then we cannot be said to behold the Lamb of God in the sense of the text. We must pray earnestly to God for his holy Spirit to guide us in the way to eternal life; this none can do but God. Let us my brethren lay up treasure in heaven, where neither moth doth corrupt nor thieves break through and steal. Matt. vi. 20-23, Seek first the kingdom of God and his righteousness and all these things shall be added unto you. And now my dear brethren, we must pray earnestly to God for the influence of his holy spirit to guide us through this howling wilderness and sea of trouble to the mansions of glory, and we should pray that God would give us grace to love and to fear him, for if we love God, black as we be, and despised as we are, God will love us. Acts x. 34, Then Peter opened his mouth and said, of a truth I perceive that God has no respect to persons. Ver. 35, In every nation he that feareth him is accepted of him. Psalm. xxxiv. 8, O taste and see that the Lord is good, and blessed is the man that trusteth in him. Ver. 15, The eyes of the Lord are upon the righteous, and his ears are open to their cry. Let us my dear brethren remember that the time is hastening when we shall appear before the Lamb of God to give an account for the deeds done in the body, when we shall be stumbling over the dark mountains of death looking into an endless eternity. O that

we may be of that happy number that shall stand with their
lamps burning. Matt. xxv. 7, Then all those virgins rose and
trimmed their lamps. Come now my brethren, let us examine
ourselves whether we have had a saving change wrought in
our hearts, and have been brought to bow to the divine
sovereignty of the most high God, and to flee to the armies
of Jesus, for he is the author of our peace, and the finisher
of our faith. Heb. xii. 2, Looking to Jesus the author and
finisher of our faith. Come now my brethren, we are one flesh
and bone, let us serve the one living and true God. Come let
us behold the Lamb of God by an eye of faith for without
faith it is impossible to please God. Heb. xi. 5, For faith
my brethren is of the things not seen. Let us my brethren
strive by the grace of God to become new creatures; for if
any man be in Christ he is a new creature, 2. Cor. iv. 17.
Let us come to the divine fountain, by constant prayer. Psal.
iv. 1, Give ear to my words O Lord, consider my medita-
tions, ver. 2, 3. Let us improve our talents by a holy life,
striving to make our calling and election sure, for now is the
accepted time; behold now is the day of salvation. 2. Cor.
vi. 2. Let us pray that God give us of the waters that the
woman of Samaria drank. John xiv. 19, But whosoever shall
drink of the water I shall give him shall never thirst, but
the water I shall give him shall be in him a well of water
springing up into everlasting life. O my dear brethren we
should be brought humbly to submit to the will of God at
all times, and to say God be merciful to us sinners, Acts iii.
19, Repent and be converted that your sins may be blotted
out. My dear brethren we are many of us seeking for a
temporal freedom, and I pray that God would grant your
desire; if we are slaves it is by the permission of God; if
we are free it must be by the power of the most high God;
be not discouraged, but cheerfully perform the duties of the
day, sensible that the same power that created the heavens
and the earth and causeth the greater light to rule the day

and the lesser to rule the night, can cause a universal freedom; and I pray God may give you grace to seek that freedom which tendeth to everlasting life. John viii. 32, And ye shall know the truth, and the truth shall make you free. Ver. 36, If the Son shall make you free, then you shall be free indeed. But as I am advanced to the age of seventy-one years, I do not desire temporal freedom for myself. My brethren, if we desire to be a happy people, we must be a holy people, and endeavour to keep the commandments of God, and we should pray that God would come and knock at the door of our hearts by the power of his holy spirit, and give us a stedfastness in the merits of Christ, and we are to believe in Christ for eternal salvation. Mr. Stoddard, a great divine, says, in speaking of appearing in the righteousness of Christ, when men believe it is part of God's covenant, to make them continue to believe. Job. vi. 12. And again he saith, since God hath promised life unto all that believe in this righteousness, it must needs be safe to appear before God in this righteousness. Jer. iii. 22, Return ye back-sliding children and I will heal your back-slidings; behold we come unto thee for thou are the Lord our God. My dear brethren let not your hearts be set too much on the pleasures of this life; for if it were possible for one man to gain a thousand freedoms, and had not an interest in the merits of Christ, where must all the advantage be; for what would it profit a man if he should gain the whole world and loose his own soul, Matt. xvi. 26. My brethren we know not how soon God may send the cold hand of death to summon us out of this life to a never-ending eternity, there to appear before the judgment seat of Christ. 2 Cor. v. 10, For all must appear before the judgment seat of Christ. And now I conclude with a few words — let me tell you my dear brethren, that in a few days we must all appear before the judgment seat of Christ, there to give an account for the deeds done in the body. Let us my brethren strive to be so prepared for death, by the grace of God, that when the time shall come when we are shaking off the shackles of this life, and are passing through the valley of the shadow of death. O may we then be enabled to say, come Lord Jesus come quickly, for thou art the Lamb of God, in whom my soul delighteth; Then my dear brethren all those which have repented of their sins shall hear this voice, come unto me. Matt. xxv. 34, Then shall the King say unto them on his right hand; come ye blessed of my Father, inherit the kingdom prepared for you from the foundation of the world. But if we do not repent of our sins we must hear this voice, Matt. xxv. 41, Then shall he say also unto them on his left hand, depart from me ye cursed into everlasting fire prepared for the devil and his angels. Then will our souls waft away into an endless eternity, and our bodies lodged in the cold and silent grave, there to remain till Christ's second coming. My brethren, we believe the word of God, we must believe this. 1 Cor. xiii. 41, Behold I shew you a mistery, we shall not all sleep, but we shall be changed in a moment in the twinkling of an eye, at the last trumpet; for the trumpet shall sound and the dead shall be raised, ver. 35, For this corruptable must put on incorruption, and this mortals must put on immortality. And now my brethren, let me persuade you to seek the Lord. Isaiah lv. 6, Seek the Lord while he may be found, and call on him while he is near; ver. 7, Let the wicked forsake his way, and the unrighteous man his thoughts, and let him return unto the Lord, and he will have mercy on him, and to our God and he will abundantly pardon. Therefore not be contented with the form of godliness without the power thereof. *Amen.*

AN
ADDRESS
TO THE
NEGROES

In the STATE of NEW-YORK,

BY JUPITER HAMMON,

Servant of JOHN LLOYD, jun, Esq; of the Manor of
Queen's Village, Long-Island.

" Of a truth I perceive that God is no respecter of
" persons :
" But in every Nation, he that feareth him and
" worketh righteousness, is accepted with him."—
Acts x. 34, 35.

NEW-YORK:

Printed by CARROLL and PATTERSON
No. 32, Maiden-Lane.

M,DCC,LXXXVII.

TO THE MEMBERS OF THE AFRICAN SOCIETY,
IN THE CITY OF NEW-YORK

Gentlemen,

I take the liberty to dedicate an Address to my poor brethren to you. If you think it is likely to do good among them, I do not doubt but you will take it under your care. You have discovered so much kindness and good will to those you thought were oppressed, and had no helper, that I am sure you will not despise what I have wrote, if you judge it will be of any service to them, I have nothing to add, but only to wish that "the blessing of many ready to perish, may come upon you."

I am Gentleman,

Your Servant,

JUPITER HAMMON.

Queen's Village, 24th Sept. 1786.

TO THE PUBLIC.

In the first impression of the following pages, printed in New-York, 1787, by Carrol and Patterson, they say:

As this Address is wrote in a better stile than could be expected from a slave, some may be ready to doubt of the genuineness of the production. The Author, as he informs in the title page, is a servant of Mr. Lloyd, and has been remarkable for his fidelity and abstinence from those vices, which he warns his brethren against. The manuscript, wrote in his own hand, is in our possession. We have made no material alterations in it, except in the spelling, which we found needed considerable correction.

THE PRINTERS.

New-York, 20th Feb. 1787.

We, the Subscribers, having had personal acquaintance with Jupiter Hammon, Author of the Address to the People of Colour in the State of New-York, believe he supported a good moral character; was much respected in his master's family, and among his acquaintance in general; and we have no doubt but the Address alluded to, is a genuine production of his own.

Arnold Fleet,
Samuel Haviland,
Fry Willis.

Oysterbay, 10th of 1st mo. 1806.

AN

ADDRESS TO THE NEGROES

OF THE

STATE OF NEW-YORK

When I am writing to you with a design to say something to you for your good, and with a view to promote your happiness, I can with truth and sincerity join with the apostle Paul, when speaking of his own nation the Jews, and say: *"That I have great heaviness and continual sorrow in my heart for my brethren, my kinsmen according to the flesh."* Yes my dear brethren, when I think of you, which is very often, and of the poor, despised and miserable state you are in, as to the things of this world, and when I think of your ignorance and stupidity, and the great wickedness of the most of you, I am pained to the heart. It is at times, almost too much for human nature to bear, and I am obliged to turn my thoughts from the subject or endeavour to still my mind, by considering that it is permitted thus to be, by that God who governs all things, who setteth up one and pulleth down another. While I have been thinking on this subject, I have frequently had great struggles in my own mind, and have been at a loss to know what to do. I have wanted exceedingly to say something to you, to call upon you with the tenderness of a father and friend, and to give you the last, and I may say dying advice, of an old man, who wishes your best good in this world, and in the world to come. But while I have had such desires, a sense of my own ignorance, and unfitness to teach others, has frequently discouraged me from attempting to say any thing to you; yet when I thought of your situation, I could not rest easy.

When I was at Hartford in Connecticut, where I lived during the war, I published several pieces which were well received, not only by those of my own colour, but by a number of the white people, who thought they might do good among their servants. This is one consideration, among others, that emboldens me now to publish what I have written to you. Another is, I think you will be more likely to listen to what is said, when you know it comes from a negro, one of your own nation and colour, and therefore can have no interest in deceiving you, or in saying any thing to you, but what he really thinks is your interest, and duty to comply with. My age, I think, gives me some right to speak to you, and reason to expect you will hearken to my advice. I am now upwards of seventy years old, and cannot expect, though I am well, and able to do almost any kind of business, to live much longer. I have passed the common bounds set for man, and must soon go the way of all the earth. I have had more experience in the world than most of you, and I have seen a great deal of the vanity and wickedness of it, I have great reason to be thankful that my lot has been so much better than most slaves have had. I suppose I have had more advantages and privileges than most of you, who are slaves, have ever known, and I believe more than many white people have enjoyed, for which I desire to bless God, and pray that he may bless those who have given them to me. I do not, my dear friends, say these things about myself, to make you think that I am wiser or better than others; but that you might hearken, without prejudice, to what I have to say to you on the following particulars.

1st. Respecting obedience to masters. Now whether it is

right, and lawful, in the sight of God, for them to make
slaves of us or not. I am certain that while we are slaves, it
is our duty to obey our masters, in all their lawful com-
mands, and mind them unless we are bid to do that which
we know to be sin, or forbidden in God's word. The apostle
Paul says: "Servants be obedient to them that are your
masters according to the flesh, with fear and trembling in
singleness in your heart as unto Christ: Not with eye service,
as men pleasers, but as the servants of Christ doing the will
of God from the heart: With good will doing service to the
Lord, and not to men: Knowing that whatever thing a man
doeth the same shall he receive of the Lord, whether he be
bond or free." — Here is a plain command of God for us to
obey our masters. It may seem hard for us, if we think our
masters wrong in holding us slaves, to obey in all things,
but who of us dare dispute with God! He has commanded
us to obey, and we ought to do it cheerfully, and freely.
This should be done by us, not only because God com-
mands, but because our own peace and comfort depend upon
it. As we depend upon our masters, for what we eat and
drink and wear, and for all our comfortable things in this
world, we cannot be happay, unless we please them. This we
cannot do without obeying them freely, without muttering or
finding fault. If a servant strives to please his master and
studies and takes pains to do it, I believe there are but few
masters who would use such a servant cruelly. Good servants
frequently make good masters. If your master is really hard,
unreasonable and cruel, there is no way so likely for you to
convince him of it, as always to obey his commands, and
try to serve him, and take care of his interest, and try to
promote it all in your power. If you are proud and stubborn
and always finding fault, your master will think the fault lies
wholly on your side; but if you are humble, and meek, and
bear all things patiently, your master may think he is wrong;
if he does not, his neighbours will be apt to see it, and will

befriend you, and try to alter his conduct. If this does not do, you must cry to him, who has the hearts of all men in his hands, and turneth them as the rivers of waters are turned.

2nd. The particular I would mention, is honesty and faithfulness.

You must suffer me now to deal plainly with you, my dear brethren, for I do not mean to flatter or omit speaking the truth, whether it is for you, or against you. How many of you are there, who allow yourselves in stealing from your masters. It is very wicked for you not to take care of your masters' goods; but how much worse is it to pilfer and and steal from them, whenever you think you shall not be found out. This you must know is very wicked and provoking to God. There are none of you so ignorant but that you must know that this is wrong. Though you may try to excuse yourselves by saying that your masters are unjust to you, and though you may try to quiet your consciences in this way, yet if you are honest in owning the truth, you must think it is as wicked, and on some accounts more wicked to steal from your masters, than from others.

We cannot certainly have any excuse, either for taking any thing that belongs to our masters, without their leave, or for being unfaithful in their business. It is our duty to be faithful, *not with eye service as men pleasers*. We have no right to stay, when we are sent on errands, any longer than to do the business we were sent upon. All the time spent idly is spent wickedly, and is unfaithfulness to our masters. In these things I must say, that I think many of you are guilty. I know that many of you endeavour to excuse yourselves, and say that you have nothing that you can call your own, and that you are under great temptations to be unfaithful and take from your masters. But this will not do; God will certainly punish you for stealing, and for being unfaithful. All that we have to mind, is our own duty. If God has put us in bad circumstances, that is not our fault, and he will not punish us for it. If any are wicked in keeping us so, we cannot help it; they must answer to God for it. Nothing will serve as an excuse to us for not doing our duty. The same God will judge both them and us. Pray then, my dear friends, fear to offend in this way, but be faithful to God, to your masters, and to your own souls.

The next thing I would mention and warn you against, is profaneness. This you know is forbidden by God. Christ tells us, "Swear not at all," and again it is said, "Thou shalt not take the name of the Lord thy God in vain, for the Lord will not hold him guiltless that taketh his name in vain." Now, though the great God has forbidden it, yet how dreadfully profane are many, and I don't know but I may say the most of you! How common is it to hear you take the terrible and awful name of the great God in vain! — To swear by it, and by Jesus Christ, his Son. — How common is it to hear you wish damnation to your companions, and to your own souls — and to sport with, in the name of Heaven and Hell, as if there were no such places for you to hope for or to fear. Oh my friends, be warned to forsake this dreadful sin of profaneness. Pray, my dear friends, believe and realize that there is a God — that he is great and terrible beyond what you can think — that he keeps you in life every moment — and that he can send you to that awful Hell that you laugh at, in an instant, and confine you there for ever; and that he will certainly do it, if you do not repent. You certainly do not believe that there is a God, or that there is a Heaven or Hell, or you would never trifle with them. It would make you shudder, if you hear others do it, if you believe them as much as you believe any thing you see with your bodily eyes.

I have heard some learned and good men say that the heathen, and all that worshipped false gods, never spoke lightly or irreverently of their gods; they never took their

names in vain, or jested with those things which they held
sacred. Now, why should the true God, who made all things,
be treated worse in this respect than those false gods that
were made of wood and stone? I believe it is because Satan
tempts men to do it. He tried to make them love their false
gods, and to speak well of them; but he wishes to have men
think lightly of the true God, to take his holy name in vain,
and to scoff at and make a jest of all things that are really
good. You may think that Satan has not power to do so
much, and have so great influence on the minds of men:
But the Scripture says, *"He goeth about like a roaring Lion,
seeking whom he may devour — That he is the prince of the
power of the air — and that he rules in the hearts of the chil-
dren of disobedience, — and that wicked men are led captive
by him, to do his will."* All those of you who are profane,
are serving the Devil. You are doing what he tempts and
desires you to do. If you could see him with your bodily
eyes, would you like to make an agreement with him to
serve him, and do as he bid you? I believe most of you
would be shocked at this; but you may be certain that all
of you who allow yourselves in this sin, are as really serving
him, and to just as good purpose, as if you met him and
promised to dishonor God, and serve him with all your
might. Do you believe this? It is true whether you believe it
or not. Some of you to excuse yourselves, may plead the
example of others, and say that you hear a great many
white people, who know more than such poor ignorant
Negroes as you are, and some who are rich and great
gentlemen, swear, and talk profanely; and some of you may
say this of your masters, and say no more than is true. But
all this is not a sufficient excuse for you. You know that
murder is wicked. If you saw your master kill a man, do
you suppose this would be any excuse for you, if you should
commit the same crime? You must know it would not; nor
will your hearing him curse and swear, and take the name

of God in vain, or any other man, be he ever so great or
rich, excuse you. God is greater than all other beings, and
him we are bound to obey. To him we must give an ac-
count for every *idle* word that we speak. He will bring us
all, rich and poor, white and black, to his judgment seat.
If we are found among those who *feared his name,* and
trembled at his word, we shall be called good and faithful
servants. Our slavery will be at an end, and though ever so
mean, low and despised in this world, we shall sit with God
in his kingdom, as Kings and Priests, and rejoice for ever
and ever. Do not then, my dear friends, take God's holy
name in vain, or speak profanely in any way. Let not the
example of others lead you into the sin, but reverence and
fear that great *and fearful name, the Lord our God.*

I might now caution you against other sins to which you
are exposed; but as I meant only to mention those you were
exposed to, more than others, by your being slaves, I will
conclude what I have to say to you, by advising you to
become religious, and to make religion the great business
of your lives.

Now I acknowledge that liberty is a great thing, and
worth seeking for, if we can get it honestly; and by our
good conduct prevail on our masters to set us free: though
for my own part I do not wish to be free, yet I should be
glad if others, especially the young Negroes, were to be free;
for many of us who are grown up slaves, and have always
had masters to take care of us, should hardly know how to
take care of ourselves; and it may be more for our own
comfort to remain as we are. That liberty is a great thing
we may know from our own feelings, and we may likewise
judge so from the conduct of the white people in the late
war. How much money has been spent, and how many lives
have been lost to defend their liberty! I must say that I have
hoped that God would open their eyes, when they were so
much engaged for liberty, to think of the state of the poor

blacks, and to pity us. He has done it in some measure, and has raised us up many friends; for which we have reason to be thankful, and to hope in his mercy. What may be done further, he only knows, for *known unto God are all his ways from the beginning*. But this, my dear brethren, is by no means the greatest thing we have to be concerned about. Getting our liberty in this world is nothing to our having the liberty of the children of God. Now the Bible tells us that we are all, by nature, sinners; that we are slaves to sin and Satan, and that unless we are converted, or born again, we must be miserable for ever. Christ says, except a man be born again, he cannot see the kingdom of God; and all that do not see the kingdom of God, must be in the kingdom of darkness. There are but two places where all go after death, white and black, rich and poor; those places are Heaven and Hell. Heaven is a place made for those who are born again, and who love God; and it is a place where they will be happy for ever. Hell is a place made for those who hate God, and are his enemies, and where they will be miserable to all eternity. Now you may think you are not enemies to God, and do not hate him: but if your heart has not been changed, and you have not become true Christians, you certainly are enemies to God, and have been opposed to him ever since you were born. Many of your, I suppose, never think of this, and are almost as ignorant as the beasts that perish. Those of you who can read, I must beg you to read the Bible; and whenever you can get time, study the Bible; and if you can get no other time, spare some of your time from sleep, and learn what the mind and will of God is. But what shall I say to them who cannot read? This lay with great weight on my mind, when I thought of writing to my poor brethren; but I hope that those who can read will take pity on them, and read what I have to say to them. In hopes of this, I will beg of you to spare no pains in trying to learn to read. If you are once engaged, you may

learn. Let all the time you can get be spent in trying to
learn to read. Get those who can read, to learn you; but
remember, that what you learn for, is to read the Bible. If
there was no Bible, it would be no matter whether you could
read or not. Reading other books would do you no good.
But the Bible is the word of God, and tells you what you
must do to please God; it tells you how you may escape
misery, and be happy for ever. If you see most people
neglect the Bible, and many that can read never look into
it, let it not harden you, and make you think lightly of it,
and that it is a book of no worth. All those who are really
good love the Bible, and meditate on it day and night. In
the Bible God has told us every thing it is necessary we
should know, in order to be happy here and hereafter. The
Bible is a revelation of the mind and will of God to men.
Therein we may learn what God is. That he made all things
by the power of his word; and that he made all things for
his own glory, and not for our glory. That he is over all,
and above all his creatures, and more above them than we
can think or conceive — that they can do nothing without
him — that he upholds them all, and will overrule all things
for his own glory. In the Bible likewise we are told what
man is. That he was at first made holy, in the image of
God; that he fell from that state of holiness, and became an
enemy to God; and that since the fall, *all the imaginations
of the thoughts of his heart are evil, and only evil, and that
continually. That the carnal mind is not subject to the law of
God, neither indeed can be.* And that all mankind were under
the wrath and curse of God, and must have been for ever
miserable, if they had been left to suffer what their sins
deserved. It tells us that God, to save some of mankind,
sent his Son into this world to die, in the room and stead
of sinners; and that now God can save from eternal misery
all that believe in his Son, and take him for their Saviour;
and that all are called upon to repent, and believe in Jesus

Christ. It tells us that those who do repent and believe, and are friends to Christ, shall have many trials and sufferings in this world, but that they shall be happy for ever, after death, and reign with Christ to all eternity. The Bible tells us that this world is a place of trial, and that there is no other time or place for us to alter, but in this life. If we are Christians when we die, we shall awake to the resurrection of life; if not, we shall awake to the resurrection of damnation. It tells us we must all live in Heaven or Hell, be happy or miserable, and that without end. The Bible does not tell us of but two places, for all to go to. There is no place for innocent folks, that are not Christians. There is no place for ignorant folks, that did not know how to be Christians. What I mean is, that there is no place besides Heaven and Hell. These two places will receive all mankind; for Christ says, there are but two sorts, *he that is not with me is against me; and he that gathereth not with me, scattereth abroad.* — The Bible likewise tells us that this world, and all things in it, shall be burnt up — and that "God has appointed a day in which he will judge the world; and that he will bring every secret thing, whether it be good or bad, into judgment — that which is done in secret shall be declared on the house top." I do not know, nor do I think any can tell, but that the day of judgment may last a thousand years. God could tell the state of all his creatures in a moment, but then every thing that every one has done, through his whole life, is to be told before the whole world of angels and men. Oh how solemn is the thought! You and I must stand, and hear every thing we have thought or done, however secret, however wicked and vile, told before all the men and women that ever have been, or ever will be, and before all the angels, good and bad.

Now, my dear friends, seeing the Bible is the word of God, and every thing in it is true, and it reveals such awful and glorious things, what can be more important than that you should learn to read it; and when you have learned to read, that you should study it day and night. There are some things very encouraging in God's word for such ignorant creatures as we are; for God hath not chosen the rich of this world. Not many rich, not many noble are called, but God hath chosen the weak things of this world, and things which are not, to confound the things that are. And when the great and the rich refused coming to the gospel feast, the servant was told to go into the highways and hedges, and compel those poor creatures that he found there, to come in. Now, my brethren, it seems to me that there are no people that ought to attend to the hope of happiness in another world so much as we. Most of us are cut off from comfort and happiness here in this world, and can expect nothing from it. Now seeing this is the case, why should we not take care to be happy after death? Why should we spend our whole lives in sinning against God; and be miserable in this world, and in the world to come? If we do thus, we shall certainly be the greatest fools. We shall be slaves here, and slaves for ever. We cannot plead so great temptations to neglect religion as others. Riches and honours which drown the greater part of mankind, who have the gospel, in perdition, can be little or no temptations to us.

We have so little time in this world that it is no matter how wretched and miserable we are, if it prepares us for Heaven. What is forty, fifty, or sixty years, when compared to eternity? When thousands and millions of years have rolled away, this eternity will be no nigher coming to an end. Oh how glorious is an eternal life of happiness! And how dreadful an eternity of misery! Those of us who have had religious matters, and have been taught to read the Bible, and have been brought by their example and teaching to a sense of divine things, how happy shall we be to meet them in Heaven, where we shall join them in praising God for ever. But if any of us have had such masters, and yet have lived and died wicked, how will it add to our misery to think of our folly. If any of us, who have wicked and profane masters, should become religious, how will our estates be changed in another world. Oh, my friends, let me intreat of you to think on these things, and to live as if you believed them to be true. If you become Christians, you will have reason to bless God for ever, that you have been brought into a land where you have heard the gospel, though you have been slaves. If we should ever get to Heaven, we shall find nobody to reproach us for being black, or for being slaves. Let me beg of you, my dear African brethren, to think very little of your bondage in this life; for your thinking of it will do you no good. If God designs to set us free, he will do it in his own time and way; but think of your bondage to sin and Satan, and do not rest until you are delivered from it.

We cannot be happy, if we are ever so free or ever so rich, while we are servants of sin, and slaves to Satan. We must be miserable here, and to all eternity.

I will conclude what I have to say with a few words to those Negroes who have their liberty. The most of what I have said to those who are slaves, may be of use to you; but you have more advantages, on some accounts, if you will improve your freedom, as you may do, than they. You have more time to read God's holy word, and to take care of the salvation of your souls. Let me beg of you to spend your time in this way, or it will be better for you if you had always been slaves. If you think seriously of the matter, you must conclude that if you do not use your freedom to promote the salvation of your souls, it will not be of any lasting good to you. Besides all this, if you are idle, and take to bad courses, you will hurt those of your brethren who are slaves, and do all in your power to prevent their being free. One great reason that is given by some for not freeing us, I understand, is, that we should not know how to take care of ourselves, and should take to bad courses; that we should be lazy and idle, and get drunk and steal. Now all those of you who follow any bad courses, and who do not take care to get an honest living by your labour and industry, are doing more to prevent our being free than any body else. Let me beg of you then, for the sake of your own good and happiness, in time, and for eternity, and for the sake of your poor brethren, who are still in bondage, *"to lead quiet and peaceable lives in all Godliness and honesty,"* and may God bless you, and bring you to his kingdom, for Christ's sake, Amen.

BIBLIOGRAPHY OF THE WORKS OF
JUPITER HAMMON

An / Evening Thought. / Salvation by Christ, / with / Penetential Cries: / Composed by Jupiter Hammon, a Negro belonging to Mr Lloyd, of Queen's- / Village, on Long-Island, the 25th of December, 1760. / Broadside of 88 lines, printed in double column, and word "Finis" at bottom. Size 10-1/4 x 7-7/8 inches.

This broadside proves conclusively that Jupiter Hammon was writing poetry in America at least nine years before Phillis Wheatley published her first work, The Elegy on the Death of Whitefield. It also proves that Hammon was without doubt the first writer of color whose work appeared in print in what is now the United States. The only copy known is in The New York Historical Society. It was probably printed at New York.

Hartford, August 4, 1778. / An Address to Miss Phillis Wheatly, (sic) Ethiopian Po- / etess, in Boston, who came from Africa at eight years of age, and / soon became acquainted with the Gospel of Jesus Christ. / (one line, followed by 21 verses of 4 lines each, printed in double column) / Composed by Jupiter Hammon, a Negro Man belonging to Mr. Joseph Lloyd, of Queen's Village, / on Long-Island, now in Hartford. /

The above lines are published by the Author, and a number of his friends, who desire to join with him in their best / regards to Miss Wheatly. (sic) / Broadside, without doubt printed at Hartford. Size 8-3/4 x 6 inches. The only known copy is in The Connecticut Historical Society.

An Essay on the Ten Virgins. Composed by Jupiter
Hammon, a Negro Man belonging to Mr. Joseph Lloyd of
Queen's Village on Long Island, now in Hartford. Hartford:
Printed by Hudson and Goodwin, 1779.

> I have been unable to locate a copy of the above. It is
> mentioned in the Conn. Courant, Dec. 14, 1779. "To be
> sold at the Printing-Office in Hartford." Although men-
> tioned by several bibliographers, none give a collation and
> all seem to take their information from the above source,
> or from Trumbull's list of Conn. imprints. Mr. Trumbull
> also obtained his information from the advertisement in
> the *Courant*.

A / Winter Piece: / being a / Serious Exhortation, with
a call to the / Unconverted: / and a short / Contempla-
tion / on the / Death of Jesus Christ. / Written by Jupiter
Hammon, / A Negro Man belonging to Mr. John Lloyd,
of / Queen's Village, on Long Island, now in Hartford. /
Published by the Author with the Assistance / of his Friends.
/ Hartford: / Printed for the Author. / M. DCC. LXXXII:
/ 8vo. pp. (2),-22-(1),-24.

> Probably printed by Hudson & Goodwin. "A Poem for
> children with Thoughts on Death." Occupies pp. (23)-24.
> Copies are in The Connecticut Historical Society and in
> The Massachusetts Historical Society Collections. Another
> is in the Providence Public Library.

An / Evening's Improvement. / Shewing, / the Necessity
of beholding / the Lamb of God. / *To which is added,* /
A Dialogue, / Entitled, / The Kind Master and / Dutiful
Servant. / Written by Jupiter Hammon, a Negro / Man
belonging to Mr. *John Lloyd,* of Queen's / Village, on
Long-Island, now in Hartford. / Hartford: / *Printed for
the Author, by the Assistance of his Friends.* / 8vo. pp.
(2),-3-28.

> Printed during the Revolution, probably by Hudson &
> Goodwin. The New York Historical Society has the copy

formerly owned by Daniel Parish, Jr. This is the only copy
I can trace.

An / Address / to the / Negroes / In the State of New-
York, / By Jupiter Hammon, / Servant of John Lloyd, jun,
Esq; of the Manor of Queen's Village, Long-Island. /
(4 lines from Acts. X. 34, 35) / New-York: / Printed
by Carroll and Patterson / No. 32, Maiden-Lane, /
M, DCC, LXXXVII. / 8vo pp. (2), -III, -IV, -(1),-6-20.

A copy is in the collection of Henry C. Sturges, of New
York. Others are in The New York Historical Society and
in The John Carter Brown Library.

The Printers of this, the first edition, make the following
statement, the wording differing slightly from that in the
Philadelphia re-issue:

"As this Address is wrote in a better stile than could be
expected from a slave, some may doubt of the genuineness
of the Production. The author, as he informs in the title
page, is a servant of Mr. Lloyd, and has been remarkable
for his fidelity and abstinence from those vices, which he
warns his brethren against. The manuscript wrote in his
own hand, is in our possession. We have made no material
alterations in it, except in the spelling, which we found
needed considerable correction.

The Printers,
New-York 20th. Feb. 1787.

An / Address / to the Negroes, / In The / State of
New-York. / by Jupiter Hammon, Servant of John Lloyd, /
jun. Esq. of the Manor of Queen's Village, Long-Island. /
(3 lines from *Acts.* X. 34, 35. / New-York Printed: /
Philadelphia Reprinted By Daniel Humphreys, / in Spruce-
Street, near the Drawbridge. / M. DCC. LXXXVII. /
8vo. pp. (3),-4-15,-(1).

Dedicated "To the Members of the African Society of
New York." Dated "Queen's Village, 24th. Sept. 1786."

On the last page is the following interesting statement:

"As this address is wrote in a better stile than could be
expected from a slave, some may be ready to doubt of the
genuineness of the production. — The Author, as he in-

forms in the title-page, is a servant of Mr. Lloyd, and has been remarkable for his fidelity and abstinance from those vices, which he warns his brethren against. The manuscript wrote in his own hand, is in the possession of Messrs. Carroll and Patterson, printers, in New-York. — They have made no material alterations in it, except in the spelling, which they found needed considerable correction. The Printer.''

Copies of this edition are in the New York Public Library, and in the Harvard College Library. A copy in the New York Historical Society has a leaf preceding the title which contains the following statement. This copy is the only one I have been able to trace which has this leaf.

"At a Meeting of the Acting Committee of the Pennsylvania Society for promoting the Abolition of Slavery, &c. June 30, 1787 — A Pamphlet wrote by Jupiter Hammon, servant to John Lloyd, jun. Esq. Queen's Village, Long-Island, and addressed to the African descendants in General, was laid before them. Impressed with a lively sense of the good effects that may result from a re-publication thereof, to those persons to whom it is particularly addressed, Ordered, that Daniel Humphreys be directed to print five hundred copies, for the purposes above mentioned.

Extract from the Minutes.

Thomas Harrison, Clerk

to Acting Committee.''

An Address to the Negroes in the State of New York. By Jupiter Hammon. New York: 1806. 12mo. pp.22.

The compiler of this list had a copy of this edition several years ago. It was printed after Hammon's death and contains an attestation by three residents of Oyster Bay as to the author's good character. Although the latest of the three known editions, it seems to be the most difficult to locate. A copy was in the New York State Library but was destroyed in the fire of 1911.